AF263261

more praise for

why surrealism matters

"Mark Polizzotti's concise introduction to Surrealism is the clearest, richest, most unflinching, and most wide-ranging survey of the movement I have ever read."

—Lucy Sante, author of *The Other Paris*

"This book brilliantly conveys the importance of Surrealism far beyond the ordinary histories of the movement. It will take the reader directly into the central excitement of Surrealism, what Polizzotti calls its 'vibrancy, dynamism, and sheer intellectual thrill.'"

—Mary Ann Caws, author of *Surrealist Painters and Poets: An Anthology*

"Mark Polizzotti makes good on his title and reveals Surrealism as a source of ongoing inspiration and energy. He's the perfect guide: clear-sighted about Surrealist misogyny and homophobia, but equally clear about its revolutionary potential. A work of commanding integrity."

—Rosanna Warren, author of *Max Jacob: A Life in Art and Letters*

"Polizzotti knows that there is no Surrealism but instead a host of surrealisms born anew every generation. He also knows the history of Surrealism, original recipe, as well as anyone, and knows that its mistakes and misfires are worth talking about. This book is worth reading—especially for those who assume they already know the answer."

—Sasha Frere-Jones, author of *Earlier*

"In his concise but wide-ranging forensic book, Polizzotti shows convincingly why Surrealism's disruptive legacy remains fresh today. This is an indispensable read for anyone interested in this revolutionary, anti-colonial movement. Outstanding."

—Partha Mitter, author of *The Triumph of Modernism: India's Artists and the Avant-Garde, 1922–1947*

"The crowning achievement of Polizzotti's lifelong engagement with Surrealism, this much-needed contemporary handbook focuses on the core insights of Surrealist thought and its applications in life and art, which remain of 'ongoing pertinence.' . . . Polizzotti reconfirms the movement's original thought that 'a true revolution of the human condition must begin with a revolution of the mind.'"

—Pierre Joris, author of *A Nomad Poetics: Essays*

"Polizzotti makes the case for Surrealism as 'a radical new means of seeing the world,' a revolution of the mind, whose anarcho-poetic assault on colonialism, capitalism, and Christo-fascism is more relevant than ever. *Why Surrealism Matters* is your passport to the Republic of Dreams."
—Mark Dery, author of *Born to Be Posthumous: The Eccentric Life and Mysterious Genius of Edward Gorey*

"'Change life,' said the Surrealists. With immense elegance and erudition, Polizzotti demonstrates that Surrealism is a living social movement forged through the collective refusal of authoritarianism, oppression, and exploitation."
—Abigail Susik, author of *Surrealist Sabotage and the War on Work*

why surrealism matters

yale

university

press

new haven

and

london

mark

polizzotti

why surrealism matters

"Why X Matters" is a registered trademark of Yale University.

Copyright © 2024 by Mark Polizzotti. All rights reserved. This book may not be reproduced, in whole or in part, including illustrations, in any form (beyond that copying permitted by Sections 107 and 108 of the U.S. Copyright Law and except by reviewers for the public press), without written permission from the publishers.

yalebooks.com/art

Portions of this book were adapted, with numerous linguistic and philosophical revisions, from talks given at the University of Texas at Dallas; the National Academy Museum; the University of Tennessee; the Metropolitan Museum of Art; and the Helix Center for Interdisciplinary Investigation, as well as from the following essays:

"In Search of André Breton" (*Agni* 40, fall 1994); "Art in Its Savage State" (introduction to André Breton, *Surrealism and Painting* [Boston: MFA Publications, 2002]); "Reality Games" (*New Republic,* May 12, 2003); "An Advertisement for Heaven" (*Sienese Shredder* 1, winter 2006); "Profound Occultation" (*Parnassus* 30:1–2, spring 2008); "The Doctor Is Unconscious: Surrealism's Freudian Slips" (*Tether* 2, summer 2016); "Breton's Smartphone: Surrealism in the Digital Age" (*Catamaran* 28, spring 2020); "The Magnetic Fields" (*4Columns,* October 16, 2020); "Slumber Party" (*Apollo,* April 2022); and "Surrealism's Children" (*Liberties*, fall 2022).

Set in Adobe Garamond type by BW&A Books, Inc.
Printed in the United States of America

Library of Congress Control Number: 2023939899
ISBN 978-0-300-28554-3 (pbk.)
eISBN 978-0-300-27386-1

A catalogue record for this book is available from the British Library.

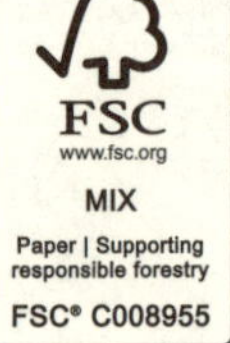

Authorized Representative in the EU: Easy Access System Europe, Mustamäe tee 50, 10621 Tallinn, Estonia, gpsr.requests@easproject.com

10 9 8 7 6 5 4 3 2 1

also by mark polizzotti

S: A Novel (in collaboration with Jean Echenoz, Harry Mathews, et al.)

Lautréamont Nomad

Revolution of the Mind: The Life of André Breton

The New Life: Poems

Los Olvidados

Bob Dylan: Highway 61 Revisited

Disordering My Library

Sympathy for the Traitor: A Translation Manifesto

Jump Cuts: Essays on Surrealism, Film, Music, Culture, and Other Utopian Topics

As editor

André Breton: Selections

Révolutions surréalistes

They Knew What They Wanted: Poems and Collages by John Ashbery

The Drunken Boat: Selected Writings of Arthur Rimbaud

For my teachers:

Jean-Louis Bouttes

Jean Gaudon

Rika Lesser

Marie-Rose Logan

Sylvère Lotringer

Linda Orr

Michael Riffaterre

Roger Shattuck

And for J.

contents

introduction: does surrealism matter?

Does Surrealism still matter? Has it ever mattered? The question is hardly new, and has been debated practically since the movement was launched. Already in 1930, a mere six years after its brash inauguration, the twenty-something poet René Daumal was cautioning André Breton, Surrealism's founder, primary theorist, and author of the *Manifesto of Surrealism* (1924), against the threat of irrelevance through popular acceptance: "Beware, André Breton, of one day figuring in study guides to literary history; whereas if we aspire to an honor, it is to be inscribed for posterity in the history of cataclysms."[1] (An apt warning, as Breton and many other Surrealists have since figured in quite a few study guides.) A dozen years later, Breton himself, in exile in the United States during World War II, fulminated to students at Yale University against the "impatient gravediggers" who declared Surrealism over and done.[2] Given that many of the young men in the audience were thinking about their looming draft notices, we can imagine that they, too, were wondering how relevant Surrealism was to their lives at that moment. And today, as Surrealism marks its centennial, and as its fortunes over the past fifty years have risen, fallen, and risen again, it's a question worth pondering once more.

Indeed, much like the students at Yale, young people of the twenty-first century could hardly be faulted for wondering what a bunch of eccentric writers and artists showing off their dream states could have to do with such pressing concerns as social and racial injustice, a faltering job market, gross economic inequities, the decimation of our civil liberties, questions of gender identity and equality, environmental devastation, education reform, or, once again as I write this, the specter of world war. All the more so in that the word "surreal" has come to stand, in the popular imagination, for a vague cluster of things, a catchall term that runs the gamut from the unnerving to the merely kooky.

The answer is that Surrealism engaged with all of these crises. To cite several examples: The Surrealists' outspoken critiques of French colonialism and racism share many points in common with current debates about racial equality and social justice. Their opposition to war and the military, dating as far back as World War I, was echoed in protests against France's involvement in Algeria and America's war in Vietnam, among others. The frankness with which they addressed sexuality, though this does not airbrush the more than equivocal position of women in the movement, was audacious for its time, and has had lasting echoes in contemporary attitudes. Their skepticism about work is almost a direct pre-echo of today's Great Resignation. In addition, their unflagging resistance to the constraints preached by the double-act of Catholicism and bourgeois morals helped pave the way for our more secular, comparatively less regulated, times. And their challenge to the rigid, rote-based educational system used in France for much of the twentieth century predates the pedagogical reforms of Piaget and Montessori. Little wonder that the Surrealist declarations spray-painted on the walls of Paris during the May 1968 student protests, though they had been coined more than forty years earlier, sounded as if freshly minted.

Even those unaware of Surrealism's influence on aspects of our social and political existence acknowledge the movement's impact on everything from fine art and literature to advertising, design, and popular culture. Without the Surrealist concept of "black humor," for instance, it's difficult to imagine the Theatre of the Absurd, Monty Python, the cinema of David Lynch, or any number of recent and current film and TV offerings. The group's practice of automatic writing feeds directly into the work of Bob Dylan, the Beats (especially William Burroughs's cut-ups), the New York School poets, and many others in their wake. Their art exhibits and demonstrations forecast the later emergence of performance art, installation art, and multimedia constructions. And Surrealist-inflected imagery has gotten so prevalent that it doesn't so much fade into the landscape as become the landscape.

Still, merely being a precursor is not enough. To my mind, Surrealism's true legacy is less as a forerunner than as a disruptor, something that perpetually challenges the existing paradigms and seeks new forms to maintain its emotional intensity. Or again, as a code-mixer, which takes in elements of its past, present, and projected future and recombines them, reworks them, reimagines them into something new, and then something newer. While some members' actions and attitudes might seem less than satisfactory, especially by current standards (which themselves will be reevaluated by future generations), I believe that their involvement with the issues listed above has much to say to the present moment, in what they got wrong as much as in what they got right.

One of Surrealism's main drivers was a refusal of the values that European society tried to force on them. As political beings, they abhorred the bellicose jingoism that came screeching to the forefront during the War of 1914–18, and they felt revulsion not only toward the war itself but also toward the societal status quo that had fostered it, as well as the economic disparities, blatant racism, and intellectual blandness that went with it. As writers and artists, they repudiated—at least in theory—the careerism and complacency that underscored so much literature and art, and that led to creative stagnation, not to say to a tacit or overt endorsement of the crumbling social contract. By nature, Surrealist works are animated by an emphatic dissociation from the reigning orthodoxy, whether political, societal, or aesthetic.

The means by which the Surrealists sought both to reject the Western world's menu of choices (its murderous oppression as well as its brain-deadening banality) and to infuse human life with a higher and more consequential meaning followed several main avenues: the search for marvels, whether through automatism, unconscious states, or the exploration of chance and coincidence; the emphasis on humor and play; the elevation of desire and sexuality into a revolutionary force; the constant search for new expressive forms, along with the transmutation of ordinary objects into objects of desire; and the reimagining of political activism not as a basic wage-and-labor program but as a much more wide-ranging liberation of the human mind. Of these, the aspect of Surrealism that to me epitomizes why it continues to resonate through changing trends and urgencies is its unwavering belief that the marvels it sought were a force for universal emancipation, within everyone's reach. The aim was to tap into previously unsuspected resources and unleash the potential we all possess for wonder, invention, and salutary rage.

With this in mind, the present book focuses on how Surrealism's varied modes of expression—verbal, visual, conceptual, political, aspirational, and experiential—participated in a design that far outstripped aesthetics, one that necessarily remains fluid and that continues to open new possibilities. Otherwise put, Surrealism's importance lies not so much in the works it produced as in the attitudes underlying them. Those who equate the movement with names such as Salvador Dalí, Joan Miró, Yves Tanguy, Paul Eluard, and Robert Desnos might find this surprising. But though Surrealism is now generally considered a movement in literature and the arts, and while its principal members indeed used artistic means, their initial impulses were mainly philosophical, political, and experimental. Breton, a former medical student who had studied neurology and psychiatry, defined it with scientific tonalities as "psychic automatism in its pure state, by which one proposes to express . . . the actual functioning of thought."[3] Surrealism in its essence tends not toward aesthetics but toward a radical new means of seeing the world, even a set of ethical guideposts.

To take this one step further, it has often been charged that, when compared with such currents as Impressionism, Cubism, or Expressionism, Surrealism yielded relatively few iconic artworks—a view most notably posited eighty years ago by Alfred Barr Jr., in the catalogue to his 1936 "Fantastic Art, Dada, Surrealism" show at the Museum of Modern Art: when Surrealism stops being "a cockpit of controversy," writes Barr, "it will doubtless be seen as having produced a mass of mediocre pictures . . . a fair number of excellent and enduring works of art, and even a few masterpieces."[4] It's true that for every melted watch and fur-covered teacup, for every *Nadja* and *Paris Peasant* and *Chien andalou,* there are hundreds of books and visual works that seem at best derivative, at worst frankly pedestrian, the stuff of which parodies are made. But is that the point? Without these so-called lesser works (and who's to judge?), we'd have a much poorer illustration of what Surrealism engendered, what it inspired, and what it made possible.

That's one challenge when gauging Surrealism's legacy. Another is its ambiguous status as, on the one hand, a mode of thinking and acting that forged pathways to liberation, and on the other, the brainchild of all-too-human individuals subject to many of the same prejudices and strictures they sought to reject. While this paradox has been readily seized upon by the movement's critics and has troubled the consciences of its boosters, it provides a valuable forum in which to discuss these issues objectively and clear-sightedly.

Yet another challenge is how much prominence to accord André Breton. Yes, it is his *Manifesto* of 1924 that stands as Surrealism's foundational document, and his autobiographical account *Nadja* (1928) as its most famous literary work. Yes, it was he who maintained the existence of the Paris group throughout his life. And the statements cited in reference to the movement are most often his, in large part because he formulated them more convincingly than anyone else: like it or not, Breton remains an unavoidable reference in any general discussion of Surrealism. At the same time, it's all too easy to draw an equation between Breton as a person and Surrealism as a current of thought. While there is a great deal of overlap, it is crucial to maintain a distinction between the ideas Breton propounded and the ways they were put into practice by him and others, how they developed on their own, and how they were transformed in directions often unintended by his initial formulations. As the Japanese Surrealist Takenaka Kyūshichi noted as early as 1930—the same year as René Daumal's warning—"True Surrealists take a step beyond Breton. They are not confined by the Surrealism of Breton's 'Manifesto.'"[5]

So while Breton appears frequently in this discussion, it is in full awareness of research that has been, and is being, done to re-envision the history of Surrealism though other lenses—specifically, to look past the largely Western European, white, male narrative that has long dominated Surrealism studies, and of which Breton and many of the best-known Surrealists are prime examples. One of my goals in the following chapters is to examine why Surrealisms (plural) matter—non-Western Surrealisms, gender-fluid Surrealisms, racially diverse Surrealisms—and in what ways these variants might be even more relevant to today's world. To fully understand their importance, however, we must first understand where they come from. The fact is that many, though not all, of these expressions took their inspiration from what Breton set in motion, even if they then followed very different paths.

In keeping with the Surrealist enterprise, which aimed at a seamless fusion of art, literature, ethics, identity, biography, politics, philosophy, attitude, and the overall business of living, the threads of various discussions will necessarily weave in and out over the course of this book. To try to cloister them, as many previous commentators have done, is to lose the essential energy of what makes Surrealism valid to begin with. Again, there are many Surrealisms, and even the movement's most dogmatic members, when trying to define it, have tended to contradict themselves, sometimes with abandon.

That said, in the interests of making this discussion not completely unintelligible, I have broken the book into rough clusters of topics: after a first chapter that seeks to provide the background and key themes, the chapter "Transformation" examines the group's quest for marvels through such means as automatism and dreams, the transformation of spaces, and the transmuting of objects and expressive forms. "Appropriation" focuses on how Surrealist techniques repurpose such pursuits as games and advertising, as well as on questions of race and of cultural absorption. The chapter "Subversion" looks at an ethics of Surrealism as it applies to personal conduct, societal norms, and the power of humor. "Transgression" interrogates questions of identity, especially with regard to sexual politics and the role of women in the movement. "Disruption" explores the balance between the Surrealists' political engagement, specifically with the Communist Left, and the desire to preserve their independence of thought and action. And "Revolution" evaluates the ongoing legacy of Surrealism and the lessons that might be drawn from the movement's successes and failures.

This book, then, is not intended as yet another history of Surrealism, nor does it claim to be comprehensive. Rather, it seeks to open a vista onto Surrealism's major concepts and aims, its impact, and, most of all, its ongoing pertinence. More than providing answers, it hopes to provoke questions and further debate. One of Breton's many attempts to encapsulate the movement's wide-ranging goals was: "Transform the world, change life, refashion human understanding from top to bottom."[6] This is admittedly a tall order, but one that arguably has kept Surrealism from ossifying into an artifact, to be dusted off every few years, set on an exhibition shelf, then shoved back in the drawer.

As it happens, that last assertion has been given a regrettable and unexpected opportunity to be tested: Conceived shortly before Covid-19 upended the world and composed in the years that followed, this book was written against a backdrop of upheavals that included a global pandemic and its resultant social disruptions; the murders of George Floyd, Breonna Taylor, Ahmaud Arbery, and too many others; an ongoing reckoning (or lack thereof) with legacies of racial injustice and gross economic disparities; stark political polarization in country after country, with the attendant specter of increasingly autocratic regimes; and, as I write, the catastrophe of war in Ukraine.

Surrealism emerged under disturbingly similar circumstances, spurred by the carnage of World War I, fueled by the political and social unrest that followed throughout Europe, and haunted by the Spanish Influenza pandemic of 1918–20. Its legitimacy and relevance were called into question many times over the following decades, and it was all but eclipsed by the advent of the Second World War and the subsequent Cold War, and by the threat of nuclear annihilation that we have in no way eliminated, merely incorporated into our daily existence. Is it coincidence that the movement is now experiencing a resurgence of interest, as evidenced by the stream of recent publications and exhibitions highlighting it as both a historical and contemporary phenomenon?[7]

When René Daumal laid the accent on the "cataclysmic" aspect of Surrealism, rather than on the writings, paintings, films, and other artifacts it was busily producing, he foresaw a crucial but, at the time, little-recognized truth: that the permanent newness and effectiveness of the Surrealist message will depend on its continued capacity to respond to the upheavals forced upon it and incite its own upheavals in return, rather than its ability to fabricate art or literary objects. More than any other intellectual current of modern times, Surrealism posited a world that could embrace, equally and indivisibly, the violence of rebellion and the passion of creation. This book aims to parse out what is living and what is dead in Surrealist ideas, what is vibrant and what stale; to evaluate why, and whether, the revolution that Surrealism sought to foment can still claim the qualifier, as one of its tracts put it nearly a century ago, of "first and always."

1 what is surrealism?

Surrealism, starting fifteen years ago with a discovery that seemed to involve poetic language exclusively, has spread like wildfire in pursuing its course, not only in art but in life. It has provoked new states of consciousness and overthrown the walls beyond which it was immemorially supposed to be impossible to see; it has—as is being more and more generally recognized—modified sensibility, and taken a decisive step towards the unification of personality, which it found threatened by an ever more profound dissociation.

ANDRÉ BRETON, *WHAT IS SURREALISM?* (1934)

Surrealism as a defined entity saw the light of day on October 15, 1924, with the publication of André Breton's *Manifesto of Surrealism,* though the movement, as yet unnamed, had actually debuted with another text five years earlier. This prequel to the *Manifesto* was the automatic prose poem *The Magnetic Fields* by Breton and Philippe Soupault, written in the spring of 1919 and published in book form in 1920. But owing to that volume's scant impact at the time and the disruption of Paris Dada in the early 1920s, the *Manifesto* now stands as the movement's official launch.

It does so all the more in that the *Manifesto* largely offset *The Magnetic Fields*' initial lack of notice. As a summons to action, it is a masterstroke, a stirringly expressed yet cannily reasoned clarion call to venture into the mind's uncharted territories. Though published by a small press, it caused an immediate hubbub in the hypersensitive world of Parisian arts and letters, creating a recognizable profile for a movement that at the time had scarcely more to boast for itself than a vague roster of little-known adherents, a temporary office space (the short-lived Bureau of Surrealist Research at 15 Rue de Grenelle), and a few obscure volumes of poetry. In this light, the flurry of activity that accompanied Surrealism's premiere in the final months of 1924, including the group's broadside *A Corpse* (which spat on the novelist Anatole France, who had just been laid to rest with state honors), multicolored stickers bearing Surrealist slogans ("If you like love, you'll love SURREALISM"), leaflets handed out in the streets, and the first issue of their house periodical *La Révolution surréaliste,* stands as nothing so much as an aggressive promotional campaign, with Breton's *Manifesto* as its lead press release.

As Breton was the first to recognize, the publication of the *Manifesto* was more concretization than origination, "the codification of a state of mind that has manifested itself sporadically in every age and in every country,"[1] and that Surrealism itself was therefore, by nature, timeless. Though the text gives thrilling new expression to a series of precepts, it also acknowledges a wide range of antecedents. These include writers and artists whose ideas and attitudes prefigured Surrealism, such as Sade, Poe, Dante, and, "in his finer moments," Shakespeare; black humorists from Swift forward; English Gothic novelists (Matthew G. Lewis's gloriously over-the-top *The Monk* was a particular favorite); the German Romantics; poets of a darker, more decadent bent, such as Charles Baudelaire and the self-styled Comte de Lautréamont (Isidore Ducasse); the Symbolists, from the poets Arthur Rimbaud and Stéphane Mallarmé to the painter Gustave Moreau; and such unclassifiables as Raymond Roussel, Alfred Jarry, and the outsider phoneticist Jean-Pierre Brisset. (Although they are not named, Breton could also have included such artists as Blake, Bosch, Coleridge, Fuseli, Goya, Max Klinger, Alfred Kubin, and Odilon Redon.)

The Surrealist movement was also inspired and honed by a

constellation of external, time-specific elements in the years preceding its launch, ranging from historical upheavals such as the wave of anarchist bombings in the late nineteenth century and the carnage of World War I, in which many of the future Surrealists served, to the emergent discipline of Freudian psychoanalysis, technological advances in transportation and communications, and such ephemera as fashion trends, popular theater and film, and common household products. Also key were the Indigenous arts of Oceania and North America (of which the Surrealists were early champions), along with the riotous tangle of avant-garde aesthetic currents, many now forgotten, that elbowed for prominence in the late nineteenth and early twentieth centuries. All of these helped shape the thought processes that brought it into being, and that have become part of the "Surrealism" we recognize today.

Breton's *Manifesto* opens with the proposition that "man, that inveterate dreamer," has been stifled by the humdrum vapidity of modern life, as imposed by centuries of Greco-Roman rationalism; and it ends with the proclamation: "It is living and ceasing to live that are imaginary solutions. Existence is elsewhere." In between, the text jumps among various registers, from the evangelistic ("The time is coming when [poetry] decrees the end of money and by itself will break the bread of heaven for the earth!") to the hyperbolic ("Surrealism is the 'invisible ray' which will one day enable us to win out over our opponents") to the blatantly tongue-in-cheek (recipes for using Surrealism "against death" and "to catch the eye of a woman you pass in the street"). It also provides the now-canonical definition of

Surrealism that has been quoted in virtually every commentary on the movement:

> SURREALISM, *n.* Psychic automatism in its pure state, by which one proposes to express—verbally, by means of the written word, or in any other manner—the actual functioning of thought. Dictation of thought, in the absence of any control exercised by reason, exempt from any aesthetic or moral concern.
>
> ENCYCL. *Philos.* Surrealism is based on the belief in the superior reality of certain forms of previously neglected associations, in the omnipotence of dreams, in the disinterested play of thought. It tends to ruin once and for all all other psychic mechanisms and to substitute itself for them in solving all the principal problems of life.

Finally, it posits Surrealism's ultimate goal as the "resolution of these two states, dream and reality, which are seemingly so contradictory, into a kind of absolute reality, a *surreality.*"[2]

Not only did the *Manifesto* set the terms for Surrealism as Breton envisioned it but, largely because of its author's artful flair for the dramatic, it was also able to fend off a rival claim to copyright of the word "Surrealism," for the term itself had a history. Coined in 1917 by the poet and cultural omnivore Guillaume Apollinaire, Breton's onetime mentor, it originally had much to do with poetic analogy and very little with "the actual functioning of thought." "When man tried to imitate walking he created the wheel, which does not resemble a leg," Apollinaire had written. "He thus performed an act of surrealism without realizing it."[3] It was this definition that the writers Paul Dermée and Yvan Goll, Apollinaire's faithful acolytes, aimed to protect from the

Breton group's infringement, and for several months the literary press ran heated exchanges between the two parties. Ultimately, it was the publication of the *Manifesto* that settled the debate in Breton's favor, suggesting that had he been a less skilled copywriter, our notion of Surrealism today would be quite different, or nonexistent. Instead, the fact that the *Manifesto* not only was a more compelling piece of writing but also proposed a stimulating new life alternative with serious philosophical underpinnings, rather than the rehashed Apollinairianisms offered up by Goll and Dermée, helped ensure that its message came through loud and clear.

That message first came through loud and clear to me when I was in my teens. Though I'd never heard of Surrealism and had only a vague awareness of even its overexposed visual works, my fledgling attempts at what I'd eventually learn was automatic writing ushered me into a world that seemed absolutely and inexplicably *right,* like the confirmation of something never seen but always known. Later, the stories told by my college professors opened up a more spectacular side of the movement's history: heroic, wild, full of humor and drama. I developed a profound admiration for the group, and in particular for Breton, whose biography I would later write. Here, I thought, were people who had clashed joyously with the miserable social constraints of their time; who, well before the Hipsters and the Beats, had refused to bow in quiet acquiescence. Surrealism struck me as a gloriously *colorful* explosion in a world mournfully etched in black and white, or as the "salubrious wind" (in Rimbaud's formulation) that could sweep away my and others' suffocating misconceptions. At least that's how it seemed.

Over time, as my knowledge of Surrealism evolved, and while the humor and drama kept its hold, I came to appreciate a much more nuanced, vastly more comprehensive enterprise, one that embraced a wide variety of domains, personalities, and pursuits. The areas of activity explored by a diversity of Surrealist groups around the world, the breadth of their concerns, and the way these concerns, their underlying commonalities and divergences, might manifest over time and place, led me to appreciate the crucial role that Surrealism had played in the development of twentieth-century thought, as well as the lessons it has to offer to the twenty-first.

Who were the protagonists of this drama? While Surrealism has often, and appropriately, been characterized as a collective adventure, it's as if some historians, blending its ever-shifting membership into a hybrid entity known as "the Surrealist," have lost sight of the fact that this collectivity was made up of distinct individuals who helped give the movement its outsized profile, and who through their actions—which ranged from the epic to the astoundingly petty—infused its history with the vibrancy, dynamism, and sheer intellectual thrill that make it so fascinating. These "diverse temperaments,"[4] as Breton described them, who often entered and exited at frenetic pace during Surrealism's five decades of organized existence, included many of the leading figures of twentieth-century modernism. A highly incomplete list (which, for now, takes into account only those affiliated with the

Paris group) includes Louis Aragon, Hans Arp, Antonin Artaud, Hans Bellmer, Victor Brauner, André Breton, Luis Buñuel, Claude Cahun, Leonora Carrington, René Char, René Crevel, Salvador Dalí, Robert Desnos, Paul Eluard, Max Ernst, Leonor Fini, Alberto Giacometti, Arshile Gorky, Julien Gracq, Valentine Hugo, Wifredo Lam, Jacqueline Lamba, Michel Leiris, René Magritte, Joyce Mansour, André Masson, Roberto Matta, Joan Miró, Benjamin Péret, André Pieyre de Mandiargues, Gisèle Prassinos, Jacques Prévert, Raymond Queneau, Man Ray, Kay Sage, Philippe Soupault, Yves Tanguy, Dorothea Tanning, and Remedios Varo, not to mention such fellow travelers and frenemies as Pablo Picasso, Marcel Duchamp, Meret Oppenheim, Tristan Tzara, Frida Kahlo, Georges Bataille, and Francis Picabia.

Of these, the most prominent, and in many ways most problematic, figure is André Breton himself. On the one hand, it was Breton who provided the theoretical and conceptual framework that allowed Surrealism to flourish as a recognizable entity. Aragon might have been more verbally dazzling, Desnos more spontaneously inventive, Eluard a more accomplished poet, Artaud a more committed fanatic, but it was Breton who commanded attention, and toward whom the others gravitated. As André Masson put it, "Surrealism existed before its definition. But all the same, the definition and site of Surrealism is André Breton."[5] It was also Breton, by all accounts endowed with great personal magnetism, who gave coherence to a fluctuating group of strong and unruly personalities for nearly fifty years. One associate remarked that "when Breton came into a room, he was always the most important person there," while another recalled the "rush of emotion at being in his presence."[6] Even Georges Bataille, a frequent antagonist, admitted that Breton had "a kind of hypnotic prestige" and "exceptional, immediate authority."[7] Like many charismatic figures, he embodied the projected desires of a community—in this case, those desperately seeking a social and psychic alternative to the rationalized chaos that had brought them to war—and the epithets most frequently applied to him (pope, magus, shaman, arbiter) underscore the elevated position he held within the group and beyond it.

The irony is that, at first glance, Breton would appear the least likely figure to sustain a movement like Surrealism. Even to his admirers, he seemed somewhat old-world, his manners and courtesies (such as his habit of kissing women's hands) like something from another era. Though by no means humorless, he could be rigid in his bearing, unforgiving in his acceptances and condemnations, and somewhat pompous. Many aspects of his life were unvarying to a fault, such as the address he maintained for his entire adult life, at 42 Rue Fontaine (today Rue Pierre-Fontaine) in Paris's 9th arrondissement; or the graphologically anomalous fact that his handwriting remained unchanged from adolescence onward. At times welcoming and inclusive, at others dictatorial and hegemonic, he was by his own admission deeply homophobic, admitting very few openly gay figures into Surrealism (René Crevel and, to some extent, Claude Cahun being rare exceptions—and even then, never very comfortably), and was ill at ease with unconventional sexual practices in general, such as the open marriage maintained by his friend Paul Eluard. He abhorred drug use, had little tolerance for nightlife or wild gatherings, and imposed many of his idiosyncrasies on his followers, including an unexplained but profound aversion to music and a penchant for green food. The term "patriarchal" inevitably comes to mind, though one Surrealist's qualification of Breton as "anti-father" might be more apt.[8]

Because of these personal contradictions, Breton has frequently been damned for not practicing what he promoted, and for the tension between the exuberant discoveries he championed and his reluctance to go too far. He pushed the boundaries, inspiring generations of adventurous minds to explore outside their known parameters, spurring himself and his colleagues into new and hazardous waters; but it was also he who tried to turn everyone back when things threatened to get out of hand. The question is, does our fascination with Surrealism persist in spite of that reticence, or because of it? Given the fates of those who lived more "surrealistically"—more than a few of whom went insane or took their own lives—we have to wonder whether Breton's tendency to hold back was precisely what allowed him to sustain the Surrealist group for almost half a century, and to ensure its legacy.

Born in 1896 to a policeman father and a harshly devout mother, Breton was raised in the industrial suburb of Pantin, just northeast of Paris. He enrolled in medical school at his parents' insistence and, when World War I broke out, he served as an orderly, studying with the renowned neurologist Jean-Martin Charcot, evaluating soldiers suffering from posttraumatic stress (then called shell shock), and discovering the work of Sigmund

Freud. A serial monogamist, he was married three times, first to the future gallerist Simone Kahn in 1921; then to the painter Jacqueline Lamba in 1934 (with whom he had his only child, the artist Aube Elléouët-Breton); and finally to Elisa Bindhoff Claro, whom he met while in wartime exile in New York, and to whom he remained married until his death in 1966.

Throughout his life, Breton avoided steady employment, often living hand to mouth on his writing, some art dealing, occasional patronage, and a smattering of short-term occupations. On the other hand, it was with (as one Surrealist described it) the regularity of an office worker that he observed the daily practice of meetings at the café with other group members. Barring unavoidable impediments, these café sessions remained a constant for Breton from 1920 until his final months of life, and continued in his honor for years afterward.[9]

Beneath the veneer of regular habits, however, Breton had an unorthodox and adventurous mind. Rebelling against the conformity of his adolescence and youth, he developed an interest early on in artistic expressions outside the mainstream, and by 1913, modernism's storied miracle year, he was far more conversant than most of his peers with Cubist painting, Symbolist poetry, and other cutting-edge currents. Rarer still at the time, he was attentive to non-Western and Indigenous arts; his earliest art acquisition, while still a lycée student, was a fertility doll from Easter Island that he bought from a returning seaman, to his parents' horror. His independence of mind led him to make common cause with the newly founded French Communist Party in the mid-1920s, and it was that same independence of mind that caused him to be among the first leftist intellectuals to break with the Party ten years later over the Moscow Trials and the aesthetic strictures of Socialist Realism. Rather than simply abandon the medical training he had reluctantly endured during the war, he used it as the basis for Surrealism's experiments with automatic writing, sleep trances, and simulations of mental disorders, taking Freud and Charcot as exemplars.

Breton was not alone in founding Surrealism, and it is significant that most of the group's activities were carried out in, and defined by, collaboration. Among the primary collaborators of the early years were the poet and novelist Louis Aragon, whom Breton met during wartime medical training and who remained his closest friend and confidant for the next decade and a half; the poet, novelist, and journalist Philippe Soupault, to whom Breton was introduced by Apollinaire; and Paul Eluard, perhaps the most renowned poet to be associated with Surrealism. Sometimes labeled the "fourth musketeer" to the triad of Breton-Aragon-Soupault, Eluard stood apart from the others by virtue of already having a family (his wife, Helena Diakonova, nicknamed Gala, would later become famous as Dalí's muse, model, and unofficial manager) and by his comparatively easy financial situation.

Other important figures in Surrealism's early days include the poet and actor Antonin Artaud, who brought (in Breton's words) a "gothic landscape pierced throughout by lightning"[10] to the Paris group; René Crevel and Robert Desnos, who contributed some of the movement's most important early writings; and Benjamin Péret, whose anticlericalism and antimilitarism, as well as his ferocious sense of wordplay, inspired some of Surrealism's most iconoclastic texts. Although the *Manifesto* mentions the visual arts only in a footnote, by the following year the group had added the painters André Masson (who bonded with Breton over their embrace of Communism, and who would share Breton's turn to Trotskyism in the late 1930s) and Yves Tanguy, both—along with Max Ernst—among the first to bring a visual dimension to the movement. By 1930, they had also welcomed the painters Salvador Dalí and René Magritte, the painter and sculptor Alberto Giacometti, the filmmaker Luis Buñuel, and others who have since become fixtures of art history.

One further name deserves to be highlighted, and that is Simone Kahn (later Simone Collinet), who was married to Breton throughout the 1920s. Though she produced virtually no artworks in the traditional sense, Kahn played a central role in Surrealism's evolution, as a generous presence who helped cement relations among the members, as the person who ensured many of the group's activities, as a gallerist who would go on to exhibit and promote a number of Surrealist artists, and most of all, from a historian's viewpoint, as an astute chronicler of the group's works and days. From her meeting with Breton in 1920 until their separation in 1929, her long, detailed letters and other texts provide much of what we know today about the origins of Surrealism proper, the workings of the Bureau of Surrealist Research, such key episodes as the sleep sessions described in the next chapter, and other essential developments. She also, to her credit, and despite the acrimony of the Bretons' divorce, kept her ex-husband's letters (the reverse cannot be said), preserving for posterity another irreplaceable, close-up view of those years.[11] Without her contribution, our understanding of Surrealism as a living phenomenon would be noticeably impoverished.

Collaboration and collectivity were an essential element of Surrealist identity. In part, this was a legacy of the European avant-garde, which had long used gatherings of the like-minded as crucibles for invention. In part, too, it simply continued the French Surrealists' personal experience of having attended events such as Apollinaire's café klatches and Dada planning sessions. But more than with any of these, collectivity played a central and formative role in Surrealist life, as a catalyst and guarantor of diverse viewpoints, as well as a barrier against individual vanity. For while it's true that, in Paris, at least, the collective revolved largely around Breton, most of the group's manifestations were determined and defined by plurality.

The most constant locus of plural activities was the daily café meeting. The café was where the members regrouped to share information and make plans, practice automatic writing, and play (or invent) games. Discussion topics revolved around current events, books read and things seen, dreams had, exhibitions to organize, real or imagined slights to avenge, and political developments to protest. Many of the movement's well-documented debates, resolutions, and expulsions happened at one or another of the café headquarters that punctuate its timeline, sporting names like the Cyrano, the Prophète, or the Promenade de Vénus. Given that the Surrealist membership was defined by strong personal affinities, a sense of shared purpose, and occasional bitter rivalries, the interpersonal dynamics at the café were intense, and by all accounts it was impossible to sit passively at these meetings (the few who did were not invited back). For many of those who attended, these gatherings were the emotional and intellectual focus of the day; those who were expelled from the group found themselves bereft, isolated, even suicidal. The writer Victor Crastre noted that the "excluded Surrealist could not help falling into an abyss of desolation because at the same time, he lost his friends, Breton's attention, and the gathering places they frequented together, and was forced into solitude, or into the mediocre games of the 'literary life.'" As Michel Leiris later explained, "People are astonished that surrealist histories often seem frightful, full of exclusions and anathemas. But that came from the fact that surrealism was a passional movement. We treated each other as lovers who argue and drag each other through the mud."[12]

And here, again, a caveat: while it's difficult to avoid using the collective terms "Surrealism" and "Surrealists" to label group events and productions, there is in fact no such thing. In the Paris group alone, not to mention the many Surrealist associations that have existed throughout the world (many long gone, some ongoing), there were divisions, schisms, and diverse viewpoints all along the line. While the collective nature was crucial, to speak uniformly of "Surrealists" in virtually any context is a misnomer, a flawed label for what was in fact a confederation of individuals united by a set of convictions and passions, but highly disparate in personality, background, aesthetic approach, and philosophical and social concerns—which also speaks to the impossibility, discussed below, of defining a Surrealist "style." Consider the term at best a shorthand.[13]

Why is the distinction important? Because the tension and energy of the group *as group* was one of the Surrealist movement's most important resources. Unlike the Romantic, Impressionist, Cubist, or AbEx artists, for instance, who shared an overall aesthetic and set of ideas but who created as individuals; unlike Dada, which mounted group demonstrations and met in cafés, but without a united sense of purpose, the members of the Surrealist cohort derived much of their energy and identity from their affiliation with the collective. And while they produced many individually signed works, these works take on their full meaning as part of the aggregate. More than any movement before it and all but a few since, Surrealism embraced the idea of association not only as a strategic advantage but as a core element of its existence. Many of its signature productions, including games, multiauthor books, and jointly curated exhibitions, would lose much of their impact as solitary endeavors. The list of Surrealist creations produced by multiple hands is long, and includes such major works as *The Magnetic Fields* by Breton and Soupault, Breton and Eluard's *The Immaculate Conception* (1930), *Ralentir Travaux* (1930) by Breton, Eluard, and René Char, numerous artist's books involving Eluard, Man Ray, Ernst, and others, and the well-known game Exquisite Corpse, discussed later.

The plural dynamic was reflected not only in the unusually high number of works created in collaboration but also in the way so many self-identified Surrealists migrated between different mediums. Breton produced collages and sculptural objects in addition to poems and essays; Leonora Carrington is equally celebrated for her paintings and her harrowing stories and memoirs; Max Ernst experimented with many visual forms (a number of which he helped develop) and wrote key theoretical texts; the poet and dramaturg Antonin Artaud also made films and visual artworks; Joyce Mansour created objects that provided a plastic counterpoint to her lacerating poems; Salvador Dalí was equally at home in painting, objects, film, and writing; and so on. Of course, many creative artists have crossed media boundaries, from Blake to Baudelaire to Bob Dylan. What differentiates the Surrealists is the sheer promiscuity and purposefulness of genre interpenetration. More to the point, within that multiplicity of mediums, the collective aspiration was manifested as a single underlying orientation: "At the present time there is no fundamental difference between the ambitions of a poem by Paul Eluard or Benjamin Péret and the ambitions of a canvas by Max Ernst, Miró, or Tanguy," Breton told an audience in 1935, specifying that each of these works aimed to confront "inner representation with that of the concrete forms of the real world."[14]

Of the many precursors cited in the *Manifesto,* the many collaborators who helped define the Surrealist collective, among the most significant is one that Breton barely mentions: Dada (1916–23), the cultural and philosophical firecracker that enlisted a number of the future Surrealists in its activities. Though Dada chronologically preceded Breton's *Manifesto,* and while the two movements are often viewed in a linear succession, the fact is that many Dada and proto-Surrealist impulses occurred simultaneously (*The Magnetic Fields,* for instance, was written the year before Dada arrived in Paris), and it is more useful to think of them, as Breton later described it, as "two alternately overlapping waves."[15]

Dada began as a loose gathering of painters, writers, and performance artists in 1916 in Zurich, where most of the initial players were keeping their distance from the war. Its primary figures include the artist Hans Arp, writer-mystic-vaudevillian Hugo Ball, singer and artist Emmy Hennings, painter Marcel Janco, and most notoriously the Rumanian poet and provocateur Samuel Rosenstock, who under the name Tristan Tzara quickly emerged as Dada's front man and polemicist-in-chief. It was Tzara's "Dada Manifesto 1918," published in early 1919, that snagged the attention of Breton and his friends. "DADA DOES NOT MEAN ANYTHING," it crowed. "*Order = disorder; ego = non-ego; affirmation = negation* . . . Every man must shout: there is a great destructive, negative effort to be made. Sweep, clean."[16] Though they in fact knew little about Dada at the time—with the war barely over, communications between Zurich and Paris were irregular at best—the message they heard in Tzara's manifesto seemed to dovetail perfectly with others that had engaged them, such as the subversive poetics of Lautréamont's *Chants de Maldoror* (1869) and *Poésies* (1870) and Rimbaud's acerbic irreverence. "What impressed me most, even more than what was said, was the quality that emanated from it," Breton later said of Tzara's manifesto: "exasperated and nervous; provocative and distant; poetic, too."[17] The future Surrealists were especially attracted to the Dadaists' absolute rejection of World War I and everything that went with it, so much like their own, as well as to their commitment to causing maximum outrage.

Excited by Tzara's text and the quasi-superhuman figure they fantasized as its author, Breton and company eagerly signed on when Tzara moved to Paris in 1920, joining in Dada performances and events, penning its broadsides, throwing punches at its brawls. But as would soon become apparent, there were significant divergences between how Tzara envisioned Dada and how his Parisian associates wished to see it. Where Dada tended toward the anarchic, the French poets couldn't escape an undertow of Cartesian order; and where Tzara was content with making his "great destructive, negative effort," Breton was more enticed by the promise of building something out of the ruins. In addition, as the spring of 1920 bled into autumn, then into 1921, the intensive series of Dada "demonstrations"—staged events that included poetry readings, musical (or noise) interludes, art displays, theater pieces, harangues to the public, and as much audience offense as possible—began to wear thin on Dada's French contingent. While Tzara saw the continual hue and cry as its own justification, Breton began to find that it had all "become stereotyped, ossified."[18] The partnership sputtered on, increasingly tense, until 1922, then tumultuously ended when the proto-Surrealists disrupted Tzara's stage play *The Gas Heart* in July 1923; the "*MoUvEmEnT DADA*" (as Tzara's letterhead styled it) succumbed soon afterward.

By that time, Breton and associates were busily devising the actions and attitudes that would define the early days of Surrealism.

Still, their interlude with Dada was more than just a detour, and two aspects in particular would leave a significant imprint on the group's subsequent profile. One, explored later, was Dada's (and particularly Tzara's) genius at publicity. The second was its internationalism: by 1920, Dada claimed branch offices in Berlin, Geneva, Madrid, New York, Zurich, and Paris. Breton later remarked that the important thing, for himself and his friends, "was that the same currents were forming in two countries [Germany and France] that only yesterday had been enemies."[19]

In geographic terms, internationalism plays the same essential role in defining and appreciating Surrealism as collectivity does on the interpersonal level. It's true that in most works about Surrealism, Paris remains first among equals, often giving the impression of Saul Steinberg's 1976 *New Yorker* cover of the world viewed from Manhattan, in which virtually everything west of the city is undifferentiated flatland. The Surrealists had even created their own version of this map in 1929, the eerily prescient "World in the Time of the Surrealists," in which Russia has taken over eastern Europe and western Europe is occupied entirely by Germany and Austro-Hungary, with Paris as its capital. But while it's easy to equate Surrealism with Paris, given not only its origins but also the seductions of the city itself and the group's many paeans to it, this tends to obscure just how broad-based the movement eventually became. After a century of largely Francocentric studies, recent research is seeking to reframe the matter, looking not so much at how the Surrealist message spread from Paris as at how its underlying impulses were re-created, reinvented, and regenerated at various times in various countries and cultures.[20]

Almost from the start, the French collective welcomed members of various national origins into its ranks, and over time included such figures as (very partially, and in no particular order) the Chilean Roberta Matta, the Canary Islander Óscar Domínguez, the Spaniards Salvador Dalí, Luis Buñuel, Joan Miró, and Esteban Francés, the Rumanians Victor Brauner and Tristan Tzara (after his reconciliation with Breton), the Serbians Marko Ristić and Dušan Matić, the Hungarians Judit Reigl and Simon Hantaï, the Greek Nicolas Calas, the Belgians René Magritte, Jane Graverol, E. L. T. Mesens, Paul Nougé, Louis Scutenaire, Irène Hamoir, Marcel Mariën, and Camille Goemans, the Egyptian Georges Henein, the Austrian Wolfgang Paalen, the Britishers Leonora Carrington, David Gascoyne, Eileen Agar, Herbert Read, Gordon Onslow-Ford, and Roland Penrose, the Czechs Vítezslav Nezval, Toyen, Jindřich Štyrský, and Jindřich Heisler, the Scandinavians Wilhelm Freddie and Max Walter Svanberg, and the North Americans Man Ray, Lee Miller, Dorothea Tanning, Philip Lamantia, Kay Sage, Jean Benoît, Penelope and Franklin Rosemont, and Ted Joans. As the movement spread around the world from the 1930s onward, the roster of non-European Surrealist groups grew exponentially, their members including César Moro, Fernando Lemos, María Izquierdo, and Frances del Valle in Latin America; Mahmoud Sa'id, and Fouad Kamel in the Middle East; Kansuke Yamamoto, Toshiko Okanoue, Takenaka Kyūshichi, and Shūzō Takiguchi in Japan; and many others. Most of these figures, while retaining a greater or lesser identification with the French group, ultimately crafted a version of Surrealism that spoke more directly to their own cultural realities.

The first Surrealist exhibit outside of France was held at the Wadsworth Atheneum in Connecticut in 1931, a mere five years after the group's initial Paris exhibition, and was soon followed by shows in Brussels, Copenhagen, Prague, Santa Cruz, and London. By the end of the movement's first decade, Surrealist groups were active to a greater or lesser extent in Argentina, Belgium, Britain, the Canaries, Chile, Czechoslovakia, Denmark, the Dominican Republic, Egypt, Greece, Japan, Peru, Rumania, Sweden, and Yugoslavia, with others forming over time in Haiti, Cuba, Martinique, Colombia, Brazil, Portugal, the Netherlands, the United States, Turkey, Syria, Thailand, and the Philippines. Meanwhile, the Paris group's major works were translated into a wealth of languages, international Surrealist periodicals proliferated (some advised by the Parisians, many others not), and exhibitions and lectures began spreading across the globe—including to North America, where people either tittered at Dalí's well-publicized antics or fulminated against the Surrealists as (in the words of Congressman George Dondero [R-Mich.]) "a horde of germ-carrying art vermin."[21]

Just as not all Surrealists were of a single mind, not all Surrealisms were of a single nature: the Czech Surrealists were more politically focused than their Parisian counterparts; British artists admired Surrealism as an idea but not as a mode of living, and were less keen on group action; Japanese poets approached automatism in a way that resonated with their own cultural history;

the Cairo-based group Art et Liberté (al-Fann wa-l-Hurriyya) applied Surrealist principles to specifically Egyptian iconography and folklore, and were arguably more advanced in championing women's rights, anticolonialism, and antinationalism; and so on. Conversely, a number of French Surrealists emigrated out of France and adopted foreign imagery and viewpoints into their own work and intellectual makeup—most notably to Mexico, which Breton once dubbed "the Surrealist place par excellence,"[22] and which became for a time home to Leonora Carrington, Benjamin Péret, Remedios Varo, Kati Horna, Alice Rahon, and Wolfgang Paalen.

Surrealism thus emerges as a truly multinational current, an energy that spreads in multiple directions and takes disparate forms, its many and diverse collectives pursuing their activities independent of the Paris group, reappropriating the techniques and productions of "official" Surrealism to their own ends. It is an international language that needs no translation, for those who are able to hear it. In this regard, one striking example of Surrealism crossing borders and cultures, as well as of its collaborative ethos and its persistence well after the Paris group disbanded in 1969, is the American Surrealist Ted Joans's thirty-foot *Long Distance* (1976–2005). A variant of Exquisite Corpse, this work was created over a span of three decades and features drawings by 123 artists and writers from many countries, including John Ashbery, Amiri Baraka, Romare Bearden, Paul Bowles, William S. Burroughs, Octavio Paz, Ishmael Reed, Larry Rivers, Betye Saar, and Wole Soyinka. In 2020, the Los Angeles–based artist and curator Lisa Bowman updated the practice, and found relief from the lockdowns of Covid-19, by creating a long-range network of Exquisite Corpses, with contributions from, among others, Jodie Foster, Robin Winters, and Richard Hell.[23] The experiment is infinitely renewable and, with the advent of digital technology, no longer even requires postage.*

Surrealism constitutes less an aesthetic movement than a state of mind. Its attempts to reinfuse language and perception, and therefore our experience of life itself, with freshness and passion stem from an impulse that is more existential than aesthetic. Nonetheless, the means by which the Surrealists sought to express this impulse often took forms that are traditionally considered literary or artistic—including that most default of Western art forms, painting. So what is it that makes a work "Surrealist"?

The epithet has been used in so many ways and applied in so many contexts that the question becomes almost impossible to answer. For some it means wild humor, for others strange and disorienting juxtapositions, for still others political insurrection and radical resistance, and for yet others the enigmatic and thrilling expanse of the dreamscape. Practically every day, my Google feed for the terms "surreal," "surrealism," "surrealist" dredges up links to visual artists whose work has only a passing acquaintance (if any) with Surrealism, films labeled "surreal" as

*Or, for that matter, other people: in 2022, Kerry James Marshall created a series of single-artist "exquisite corpse" paintings, titled as such, that reference or pastiche numerous styles and paintings by other artists in each work's four disparate parts.

a synonym for "indie" or "weird," or books with slightly unusual narrative conceits. And of course, political and social events by the dozens have been tagged "surreal," especially in the current moment—a moment that also offers us "surrealist food," "surrealist tableware," "surrealist shoes," "surrealist home décor," "surrealist makeup artists," and a "surrealist winter camp" for children, while the AI tool DALL·E "creates instant Surrealist art" from a typed-in string of random words, and a flavor of Coca-Cola promises to "bottle up the technicolor tastes and surrealism of the subconscious" (does technicolor work in a blind taste test?).

One factor making it hard to distinguish a typical Surrealist work is the ever-evolving nature of what Surrealist art and writing were meant to be. While the group's initial experiments, by Breton's own admission, were "more or less limited to the poetic domain," over time their "field of investigation widened considerably."[24] In the earliest theoretical texts, such as Breton's *Manifesto* and Aragon's essay "A Wave of Dreams" (both 1924), "Surrealism" is used interchangeably with "automatism." Breton later stressed the role of unconscious thought in the creation of a Surrealist work by declaring that "any form of expression in which automatism does not at least advance *under cover* runs a grave risk of moving out of the Surrealist orbit."[25]

This held for both the verbal and visual languages. Early on, André Masson and Robert Desnos began producing automatic drawings and paintings, seeking to translate the unconscious flow in plastic terms. Max Ernst experimented with nondirective techniques, such as frottage (rubbings of floor boards and other textured surfaces) and, especially, collage, in which disparate visual elements come together in unexpected juxtapositions. As he described it: "A readymade reality . . . (an umbrella), suddenly found in the presence of another very distant and no less absurd reality (a sewing machine), in a place where both must feel *out of place* (on a dissecting table), will be robbed of its naïve purpose and of its identity [and transformed] into a new absolute, poetic and true: umbrella and sewing machine will make love."[26] Similarly, Man Ray sidestepped the photographer's agency in framing and shutter speed with his Rayographs: placing objects directly on photosensitive paper and letting the image develop unmediated, thereby giving it an entirely new life. Others, including Ernst, Óscar Domínguez, and Marcel Jean, practiced decalcomania, in which ink or paint is spread on a surface, then transferred while still wet onto another surface to create random patterns that could be interpreted in different ways.

Nonetheless, automatism alone is an inadequate criterion for Surrealism's widely varied plastic productions. Indeed, how do we square such hobbyhorses as Dalí's melting watches, Oppenheim's fur-covered cup and saucer, and Magritte's levitating, bowler-hatted burghers with the vast range of other works to which the Surrealist label is generally affixed, like Claude Cahun's gender-bending photographic self-portraits, or Alberto Giacometti's assemblages of the early 1930s, or Leonora Carrington's ghostly matriarchs, or Hans Bellmer's sado-misogynistic *poupées,* or the solarized exposures of Man Ray, Lee Miller, and Raoul Ubac, or Yves Tanguy's submarine vistas, or abstractions by Adrien Dax, Jean Degottex, and Jean-Paul Riopelle? The breadth of approach, medium, and visual impact make a properly "Surrealist" aesthetic an ever-shifting target. Indeed, for the writer Jean Schuster, it was precisely "the diversity in facture characterizing these works"[27] that preserved Surrealism from being considered a school. (In this regard, the designations of "current" or "movement," which underscore the fluid nature of Surrealism's pronouncements and productions, offer a closer approximation of how to think about it.)

It was along similar lines that Breton noted that a work of art can be considered "Surrealist" not by its particular technique but by its ability to externalize a "*purely internal model.*" What intrigued him was the artist's inner vision, the ability to make visible that "*which is not visible,*" rather than the skill with which line or color was applied to paper or canvas. "It is impossible for me to envisage a picture as being other than a window," he wrote in 1925, adding, "my first concern is then to know what it *looks out* on." In other words, in order to be Surrealist, a work of art must explore a mental space outside the field of normal awareness, in a place where consciousness and unconsciousness, the possible and the impossible, become one. Any other art—art as it was traditionally practiced—is relegated to the status of "imitation," "inexcusable abdication," a "lamentable expedient," or, as Duchamp had dismissed it, "retinal." Instead, the work must appeal to the eye as it "exists in its savage state."[28] Some years later, Breton broadened the definition: "What makes a work of art a Surrealist one is, first and foremost, the spirit in which it was conceived."[29]

Such a criterion might seem frustratingly open-ended, but it also offers a point of entry into the Surrealist universe. Boiled down to their simplest elements, Surrealist productions and actions are defined less by form or medium than by spirit and intent. While art movements have tended historically to be about the beauty or quality of the object produced, Surrealism produces art as a means rather than an end. Moreover, though it did introduce a new visual language, it differs from standard avant-gardes in its refusal of originality and newness for their own sake. Historian Michael Richardson rightly notes that "Surrealism's vitality over such a long period is no doubt due to the fact that it did not embrace the modernist cult of innovation but instead engaged with a set of complex philosophical and anthropological issues, which gave artists leeway to approach it in multiple ways relevant to their particular circumstances without being bound by what had come before."[30] The avant-garde pushes the boundaries of aesthetics toward ever renewed expressive forms; Surrealism tends instead to use forms, new *or* traditional, as tools with which to express a particular spirit. This spirit, which infuses Surrealism's varied manifestations, from creative works to political militancy, is above all one of dissidence and defiance, subtended by a belief in the inexhaustible capacity for wonder that resides in each of us, here and now.

This is where art-centered critics and historians like William S. Rubin, who curated the landmark Surrealism retrospective at the

Museum of Modern Art in 1968 but who valued the movement mainly as a forerunner of Abstract Expressionism, or Clement Greenberg, who rejected Surrealist painting as "academic art under a new literary disguise," miss the mark. By constantly seeing the Surrealist creator as setting out, as Rubin put it, "from some definition of art,"[31] these commentators keep their eye focused on the movement's formalist aspects, gauging it in precisely the "retinal" terms that Duchamp derided. Meanwhile, to paraphrase Breton, Surrealism is elsewhere.

2 transformation: the search for marvels

The image is a pure creation of the mind. It cannot be born from a comparison but from a juxtaposition of two more or less distant realities. The more the relationship between the two juxtaposed realities is distant and true, the stronger the image will be—the greater its emotional power and poetic reality.

—PIERRE REVERDY, *NORD-SUD* (1918)

If the multifarious Surrealist program could be summarized in a single endeavor, it would be the attempt to reinfuse modern life, and modern living, with the lost capacity for marvels—a capacity that they saw as essential for human thriving, but that had withered under the centuries-long procession of rationalist, religious, capitalist, and consumerist constraints, to the point where the "inveterate dreamer" Breton invoked in the *Manifesto* no longer knew which way was up. As he summarized it, "Let us not mince words: the marvelous is always beautiful, anything marvelous is beautiful, in fact only the marvelous is beautiful."[1]

Surrealism was founded on a staunch resistance to the world as it is, but this resistance went hand in hand with a firm belief in what *might be.* This was not some sort of pie-in-the-sky, 1930s sci-fi utopia, or socialist tomorrows that sing, for in the Surrealist worldview, "what might be" already exists, and "heaven," however defined, is not the site of some spiritualist or religious afterlife but part and parcel of our own daily being: the trick is to recognize it, leave oneself open to it. "We want, and will have, the 'beyond' in our time," Breton stated early on. "For this to happen, we must listen only to our own impatience, and must stand ready, with no hesitation whatsoever, to obey the marvelous"—a sentiment later echoed by the Martinican Surrealist Suzanne Césaire when she counseled, "Be in permanent readiness for the marvelous."[2] The openness to marvels is a matter not just of passive receptivity but also of active engagement, revelation, and transformation.

A frequently recurring term in Surrealism is *trouvaille:* fortuitous discovery, chance encounter, or lucky find. It touches fingers with what Freud termed the "uncanny" (*unheimlich*), occurring when "infantile" or "primitive" beliefs collide with our rationally conditioned dismissals of them, in ways that we can't immediately resolve and are forced to experience viscerally. In painting, one example of the uncanny is Pierre Roy's para-Surrealist canvas *Danger on the Stairs* (1927 or 1928), which depicts a diamondback snake slithering down an eerily quiet, disturbingly ordinary apartment staircase. A sense of the uncanny seeps through a number of horror films, from F. W. Murnau's *Nosferatu* (1922; one of the group's favorites) and Carl Theodor Dreyer's *Vampyr* (1932) to modern "rubber reality" flicks like Wes Craven's *Nightmare on Elm Street* franchise. Breton evokes a similar phenomenon in *Nadja* vis-à-vis the public statue of Etienne Dolet, which "has always fascinated me and induced unbearable discomfort"[3]—a feeling familiar in its unfamiliarity to anyone who has suddenly felt out of place in a site or situation that would normally seem anodyne. While the *trouvaille* can take an infinite number of forms, in almost every instance it combines elements of the quotidian with the unexpected, inexplicable, and disorienting, but also the oddly pleasurable. Breton described such moments as eliciting "a physical sensation . . . like the feeling of a feathery wind brushing across my temples."[4]

In pursuit of that feathery wind, the Surrealists engaged in numerous experiments, ranging from the extravagant to such seemingly commonplace exploits as seeking natural marvels in butterfly patterns and mineral formations. And they walked through the city, leaving themselves receptive to what Henry Miller called "accident and incident, drama, movement. . . . A harmony of irrelevant facts which gives to your wandering a metaphysical certitude." Breton's essay "The New Spirit," for example, recounts how he, Aragon, and the painter André Derain, while en route to meet one another, all chanced upon one striking woman, but in incongruous situations and different parts of town.[5]

Marvels might occur spontaneously or they might be there for the creating, and in the Surrealist universe, one of the best places for creating them—notwithstanding the movement's internationalism—was Paris. If Paris retains such pride of place in the history of Surrealism, it's not merely out of cultural self-reference. For many Surrealists of all nationalities, the city, particularly its mysterious byways (of which there were more a century ago), abounded in discoveries and delights, favoring explorations that often take on the character of dreams. In the automatic poem "Sunflower" from 1923, Breton conjures "a farm [that] prospered in the heart of Paris"; he later credited the poem with having predicted his meeting with Jacqueline Lamba and their amorous midnight stroll through Les Halles produce market eleven years later.[6] Aragon, one of the capital's most assiduous walkers, reimagined the city in his 1921 novel *Anicet ou le Panorama* as "a lovely erector set. . . . The Obelisk made the Sahara grow on Place de la Concorde, while galleons sailed along the rooftops of the Navy Ministry." In the aptly named *Paris Peasant* (1926), he takes the reader on an initiatory exploration of the *passages* (covered gallerias, many now demolished) in the city's northern arrondissements, metamorphosing the tawdry storefronts into palaces of wonder; and he recounts a night spent with Breton wandering through the closed Buttes-Chaumont park, "their Mesopotamia for one half-hour."[7] Others, such as Soupault in *Last Nights of Paris* (1928), have left breadcrumb trails of their perambulations throughout the French capital in search of the arresting and arousing.

One reason that Paris remains the locus classicus of Surrealism is that the Surrealists were so successful in transforming the city into more than itself, and not only in books. The aim was to induce what the French call *dépaysement* (disorientation; literally: un-countrying) in the midst of the familiar, to create a foreign country out of what they saw every day, to make home unheimlich. Patrick Waldberg recalled the painter Jacques Hérold meandering through the "gray streets" of Paris, absorbing "the tiniest details of the spectacle he chanced upon . . . enchantify[ing] the surroundings at will, transforming with a wave of his magic wand a tuft of grass into a flowering prairie, the moss on an old wall into an arid pampa, the sand of a playground into an Oceanic shore."[8] In 1933, the group launched a survey on "certain possibilities of irrationally beautifying a city," asking whether one should "preserve, displace, modify, transform, or remove" some thirty Paris monuments. The answers, ranging from "cover it in manure and blow it up" to "replace it with a can of asparagus,"[9] might seem glib, but behind the humor lies a desire to reinvent the cityscape, see it through new eyes, infuse it with an eroticism and excitement all its own: beneath the paving stones, the dream. The attempt is less quixotic than it might first appear, moreover, if we consider the points of comparison between these inquiries and current plans to create pedestrian spaces and painted streetscapes in urban areas, or debates over how and whether public monuments deemed offensive should be replaced, and with what. What seems evident is that, for such marvels to be encountered, a landscape must offer hidden corners, uncontrolled spaces—the kinds of areas that gentrification and the homogenizing mediocrity of corporate real estate interests seem bent on erasing. (That's putting it in a modern context, but Baudelaire was also deploring Haussmann's urban renewal of Paris in the mid-nineteenth century.)

Ultimately, the specific site of the Surrealists' efforts and explorations—the actual cities and streets they explored, the structures that fascinated them, the particular coincidences that fed their accounts—are of secondary importance, serving mainly to give color and sound to our bewitching mental movie of the movement's history. What matters is the adventure sought, the desire to extract a sense of wonder and uncanny delight from the banal scape, regardless of place, time, or circumstance, 1920s Paris or 2020s Paramus.

Among the best-known terrains for scavenging marvels was the exploration of dreams. Breton in particular had been impressed by Freud's writings on dreams, which were just becoming known in France at the time of his medical internship, and by the Austrian's skill in capturing their aura. While the importance of dreams in probing the deep recesses of the psyche did not escape them, the Surrealists mainly looked to hypnagogic and oneiric imagery to convey a disorienting verbal or pictorial atmosphere. They were among the first to publish dream narratives outside of a medical context, as experiences unto themselves, well before dreams became standard elements of fiction and film. One such narrative begins:

> I was sitting in a metro car opposite a woman I hadn't especially noticed when the train stopped and she got up, and looking straight at me said: "Vegetative life." I hesitated a moment—we were at the Trocadéro station—then I got up, having decided to follow her.
>
> Once at the top of the stairs, we were in an immense meadow where a late afternoon greenish daylight fell, extremely harsh . . .[10]

A primary goal in exploring dreams was to abolish the dichotomies between sleep and wakefulness, as a means of reaching the "kind of absolute reality" promoted in the *Manifesto.* Sometimes, however, this intermingling took on a dangerous life of its own. In his book *Communicating Vessels* (1932), Breton relates the unnerving experience (which he described as a "psychoanalysis of reality") of being unable to distinguish between dream and waking states during a particularly painful time in his life: the resulting onrush of coincidences, and the extrarational delirium of interpretation they inspired in him, give the narrative—though purportedly a faithful relation—an otherworldly, ungraspable character that colors his diurnal existence with twilight hues. Beyond this, portraying dreams was not only about conveying one's own mental state but also a way of tapping into the dream associations of the reader or viewer, analogous to what Jung termed the collective unconscious: a way, in other words, of both capturing and provoking that "feathery wind." A twenty-first-century update is provided by the subreddit r/thomastheplankengine, which creates "memes from your dreams," connecting users with their unconscious via more contemporary media.[11]

Analogous to the intermingling of dreams and wakefulness is the Surrealists' attunement to what Breton called "petrifying coincidence" (later rebaptized "objective chance"), an acknowledgment of the jarring concordances and electrifying encounters that potentially exist all around us, and that often have life-transforming consequences. Breton's writings offer numerous examples of such encounters. Most famously, his autobiographical narrative *Nadja* pivots on just such an event, the chance meeting in the street with a young woman who seemed to live at "the extreme limit of the Surrealist aspiration,"[12] and who indeed transformed the author's life, from his amorous situation to his way of writing to his thinking about such coincidences. Drawing an explicit connection between the thrill of encounter and that of sexual attraction, the Chicago-based Surrealist Penelope Rosemont describes objective chance as "desire precipitating reality," and goes on to say: "Much more than mere coincidences, such encounters can and do shape decisive events in our lives. The experience is a little like paranoia, but in a pleasurable form: an acute awareness that more is going on around us than we realized, but that we are actively involved in it all, and that our desire is a crucial factor."[13]

Despite the Surrealists' courting of spellbound states, one common means of attaining them, narcotics, found comparatively little favor in the group. There were those who experimented with mind-expanding drugs, such as Antonin Artaud (who considered opium a legitimate "means by which man tries to cleanse himself of despair")[14] and the members of the splinter group Le Grand Jeu; but by and large, whether because of Breton's abstemiousness or otherwise, that particular "artificial paradise" never played the determining role in Surrealism that it had with Baudelaire and Rimbaud, or that it later would with the Beats and sixties counterculture. In the *Manifesto,* Breton had written that Surrealism "acts on the mind very much as drugs do; like drugs, it creates a certain state of need and can push man to frightful revolts."[15] For him, apparently, that was mind-altering enough.

One could raise the objection that a reality illuminated by desire, dreams, and marvels sounds utopian, if not patently naïve, but there was a concrete purpose to it. As with the Surrealists' political engagements, the aim was to forge a more fulfilling, less iniquitous, less soul-draining existence. Is it really so naïve to envision how a society *not* governed by workaday necessities or the rule of money, *not* subject to obtuse and oppressive ruling structures, *not* bound by the logical, moral, and sexual strictures that have been in force for centuries, *not* given to knee-jerk aggressions (which, taking their cue from Freud, the Surrealists saw as the price of repressing our libidinous impulses), *not* dedicated to keeping people in line and their brains "doped with religion and sex and TV," as John Lennon put it, might in fact allow for greater human well-being? Given our current state of affairs, how much do we have to lose?

It's no surprise, given the predominantly writerly orientation of many Surrealists, that their means of stoking marvels frequently involved language. Eluard and Péret "updated" 152 proverbs, giving stale clichés new life by twisting familiar locutions such as "*Il faut battre le fer tant qu'il est chaud*" (Strike while the iron is hot) into "*Il faut battre sa mère pendant qu'elle est jeune*" (One must beat one's mother while she is young). Mimi Parent's mailbox-object *Boîte alerte* bends the near-homophonic *boîte à lettres* (letterbox) into an "alerter box." Michel Leiris's lexicon "Glossaire: j'y serre mes gloses" (translated by Lydia Davis as "Glossary: My Glosses' Ossuary") provides sound-based "definitions," such as "*Eclipse—ellipse de clarté*" (Eclipse—ellipsis of clarity) and, playing on the homophony in French between dreaming and revolt: "*Révolution—solution de tout rêve*" (Revolution—solution of every dream). If indeed, as Wittgenstein and others have argued, the meaning of words derives not from things but from convention, then the Surrealists intended (paraphrasing Verlaine) to take convention and wring its neck, precisely by appropriating familiar language and making it strange.[16]

The most frequently used and best known of these verbal tools was automatic writing. In the *Manifesto,* Breton described the power of words occurring from out of nowhere, or from what Victor Hugo had dubbed "the mouth of shadows":

> One evening . . . before I fell asleep, I perceived, so clearly articulated that it was impossible to change a word, but nonetheless

> removed from the sound of any voice, a rather strange phrase which came to me without any apparent relationship to the events in which, my consciousness agrees, I was then involved, a phrase which seemed to me insistent, a phrase, if I may be so bold, which was *knocking at the window.*[17]

The fascination was easy to understand: automatic expression, phrases coming unbidden, "unencumbered by the slightest inhibition," seemed a royal road to the true workings of the unconscious mind and a release from the strictures imposed by society, religion, and education. More than this, these phrases "knocking at the window" and the rarified images they evoked offered an entrance into the prime matter of language itself.

Automatic writing had been practiced in literature since at least the eighteenth century by the likes of Horace Walpole and Thomas Carlyle, and in the nineteenth by Gérard de Nerval. In psychiatry, it had been employed by such pioneers as Pierre Janet and Breton's onetime teacher Charcot; Breton in fact first came across the use of automatic speech as a psychiatric tool while treating shell-shocked patients. As with dreams, however, his enthusiasm for it, and for the unorthodox phrasings and imagery it unleashed, was neither as a literary technique nor as a therapeutic means of reinserting the analysand into functioning society.

Rather, automatism, which Breton described as "akin to *spoken thought,*" was attractive for its disruptive potential, as a generator of marvelous transformations, and he approached the practice with scientific fervor. His aim was to refresh language, to free it from the tyranny of standardized meaning and save our linguistic faculties from the banalizing functions to which the modern industrial world endlessly reduced it. By electrifying dull linguistic conventions, the Surrealists aimed to use words not to reproduce reality but to create a new and better reality. Breton later cited the example of Apollinaire, who "came much closer than anyone to thinking that in order to better the world it was not enough to rebuild it on a more equitable social basis but that it was also necessary to temper with the essence of the Word."[18] This was a conviction that would follow him throughout his life, and that would largely define the grandeur and difficulty of the Surrealists' attempts at social activism.

In *Essay on the Origin of Languages,* Jean-Jacques Rousseau contends that "the first invention of speech is due not to the needs but to the passions"—otherwise put, that the proper function of language is emotional rather than pragmatic. Breton's proclamation in the *Manifesto* that "language has been given to man so that he may make Surrealist use of it,"[19] breezy as it might sound, follows a similar line of thinking: that language springs from a place much deeper in our beings than is suggested by the uninspired use to which we generally put it. Automatism becomes a way of transforming language from a utilitarian sawhorse into a thing of wonder. Aragon furthered the point when he asserted that "the meaning of words is not a mere matter of dictionary definition," as did Magritte, when he insisted that "there is little connection between an object and what depicts it": the image of a pipe is not, in fact, an actual pipe, and a leather bag might just as well be captioned "the sky."[20]

Given the spontaneous nature of the utterances, the fact that automatism is "within everyone's reach," and the collaborative generation of many of the texts, automatic writing also undercuts the vanity of individual authorship. Breton labeled it an attempt to "adapt a moral attitude, and the only one possible, to a writing process."[21] The first illustration of this was the prose poem sequence *The Magnetic Fields,* which Breton co-wrote with Philippe Soupault. The manuscript was produced over the course of eight intense days in the spring of 1919, its two authors cloistered in a hotel room and coaxing phrases from the "mouth of shadows" through various means, including writing in an uninterrupted flow and holding spontaneous rapid-fire dialogues. Their hastily scribbled sheets jumbled together fancy, personal reminiscence, incongruous juxtapositions, and phrases that still sound fresh a hundred years after the fact: "You know that tonight there is a green crime to commit" (a remarkable number of phrases in the book suggest crime or danger). "Cathedral sweat superior vertebrate." "The operator, in order to photograph certain plants, is obliged to hold a fan and must pretend to be dancing." "Stiff stalk of Suzanne uselessness especially village of flavors with a lobster church."[22] The text is also peppered with stock phrases, advertising slogans, deformed locutions, and pastiches of such admired predecessors as Rimbaud, Apollinaire, and Isidore Ducasse (Lautréamont), whose credo in *Poésies,* "Poetry must be made by all. Not by one,"[23] anticipates *The Magnetic Fields*' pluralistic conception by decades, and the sampling aesthetic by nearly a century.

Automatic writing was not without its detractors: Aragon, for one, noted that its use quickly became "stereotyped," and warned that "if you write deplorable twaddle using Surrealist techniques, it will still be deplorable twaddle. No excuses"[24]—a charge that anyone who has slogged through pages of texts by writers who lacked the talent of a Breton, an Aragon, a Desnos, or a Péret might find hard to refute. Breton himself, despite his initial enthusiasm, came to despair of automatic writing in the mid-1930s as a "continual misfortune," prey to devolving into a mere literary technique that "the vanity of certain authors" had tainted. Nonetheless, he maintained his faith in automatism in general as a key element of Surrealist activity, celebrating its ability to cast "light upon the unrevealed and yet revealable portion of our being."[25] His last book of poems, *Le La* (1961), was composed entirely of four automatic sentences, bringing him full circle to the phrases that had knocked at his window more than four decades earlier.

Delving into the unconscious could prove disappointing, but it could also prove patently hazardous. Breton had cut short the writing of *The Magnetic Fields* after a week, fearing for his and Soupault's mental equilibrium; he later recounted that one phrase in the book, "Tires velvet paws," had caused him to spend an afternoon feeling stalked "by cats who were perhaps (but please believe me: only perhaps) cars."[26] The hazards became still more evident three years later, when René Crevel introduced the group to hypnotic slumbers.

Hypnotism, trances, and seances were a common feature of spiritualist practice, a way of connecting with the dead through the agency of supernatural forces. For Breton and his circle, however, they had nothing to do with hearing from the Beyond, nor were they some sort of parlor game. Rather, they were another means, like automatic writing, like dreams, of probing human expressiveness, tapping into thoughts and imagery that regular consciousness seemed unable to access. By forcing sleep, these young poets were looking to wake up.

At first, the sessions seemed to bear out their wildest hopes. Crevel fell into a deep trance, heaving "hoarse sighs and vague exclamations," as Simone Breton recounted with a shudder, and telling "a gruesome story in a forced, declamatory tone. . . . Painful, cruel accents. Savagery in every image. Some obscenity as well. . . . Nothing can match the horror of it." On subsequent evenings, other participants demonstrated equal susceptibility to hypnosis. Robert Desnos, who claimed to be in telepathic communication with Marcel Duchamp (then in New York), disgorged a flood of inventive spoonerisms that mirrored Duchamp's own wordplay. Others made chilling predictions—which then came true, leaving the participants "crazy with terror"—or cried out in horror at visual or tactile hallucinations, or flailed about on the floor, or barked like the Bretons' dog and proceeded to eat from the animal's dish. Those present were mesmerized, the effect on them so powerful that the sessions soon began taking on the earmarks of addiction. As Simone reported to her cousin, "After each séance, we're so dazed and broken that we swear never to start up again, and the next day all we can think about is being back in that catastrophic atmosphere."[27]

Before long, however, the catastrophe threatened to become not merely atmospheric but actual: Crevel tried to orchestrate a group suicide among the hypnotized guests. Desnos chased Paul Eluard around the lawn brandishing a carving knife. Crevel and Desnos also fell into a competition for Breton's notice that quickly turned violent, leading Crevel to realize "that I am going to lose my life or at least my head if I go on," while Breton tried in vain to wean Desnos off the sessions, "fearing that his personal faculties wouldn't bear up."[28] After further escalations, he terminated the experiment once and for all.

Despite such dangers—or because of them?—it is tempting to try to recapture today the exhilaration the early Surrealists felt, the thrill of venturing into a wholly new experience. But what does that mean? While one could, for instance, write automatically just as easily on a laptop in Starbucks as with a fountain pen on Paris café stationery, the modern writer's efforts carry a weight of historical precedent that the original Surrealists' did not (a conundrum that was already afflicting Surrealists of the postwar generation). More to the point, the shared set of cultural and literary references that allow for our spontaneous understanding of automatic writing have changed—to be replaced not by other shared references but rather, in an age when syllabi and credences have become less standardized, by a much more diffuse corpus. When Jacqueline Chénieux-Gendron notes that "automatic writing responds to a system of thought that no longer makes sense . . . now that handwriting is disappearing, as is the rote memorization-based education that formed the basis of the Surrealists' verbal inspiration,"[29] she is targeting not only the generative mechanism of automatism but also our understanding of it as receptors.

In one of his most aspirational statements, Breton identified the ultimate goal of automatism, and of Surrealism in general, as finding and fixing "a certain point of the mind at which life and death, the real and the imagined, past and future, the communicable and the incommunicable, high and low, cease to be perceived as contradictions."[30] If the practice of automatism remains at all relevant today, it is not about re-creating the conditions that the Surrealists invented in the 1920s, which would be derivative and no doubt pointless, but rather of reconnecting with its energy, its power to reveal new forms of thinking, new ways of seeing, conveying, desiring. While the principle of automatism remains vibrant, its execution needs constant reinvention. The Surrealists were not out to escape the world via automatic trances and dreams but to reimagine a better one than centuries of Greco-Roman logic, with its strict categorical divisions, had managed to produce. The fact that pursuits such as automatic writing and sleep seances instinctively strike us today as frivolous is only one pernicious result of this rationalist conditioning.

While poetry is considered Surrealism's main mode of literary expression, the movement also had a transformative impact on prose. Works such as Breton's *Nadja* and *Mad Love* (1937), Aragon's *Paris Peasant,* Crevel's *Putting My Foot in It* (1933), and Leiris's *Manhood* (1939), all of which combine, to varying degrees, autobiography, ethnography, sociology, and philosophical reflection, stand at an ever-shifting point between novel, memoir, reportage, and essay, without ever quite fitting into any of those categories. They can be seen as direct precursors of the New Journalism and contemporary metafictions and autofictions. Furthermore, as Chénieux-Gendron has pointed out, Breton's insertion of disparate quotes and paraphrases into his own work creates a network of connections and allusions over an entire constellation of thought, establishing "bridges" between the assembled fragments[31]—a process that seems more akin to Web-surfing than to linear reading.

One of Surrealism's most significant literary contributions might well be its radical renovation of critical prose. Containing a heady mix of personal reminiscence, flight of fancy, scattershot association, delirium, and shrewd analogy, much Surrealist criticism demands to be experienced rather than described, and puts instinct and feeling before the rational exposition of most discursive writing, even at the expense of intelligibility. Breton, who once unmasked a fake Rimbaud poem solely on the basis of instinctive affinity (after virtually every connoisseur had been duped), summed it up: "The point is not to understand but to *love.* Or at least, the gaps in comprehension do not matter, or might even be desirable in allowing the vibrations of the heart to flow through comprehension unhindered."[32] Not to say that the Surrealists didn't know their stuff; but by putting intuition before erudition, they claimed a more immediate access to beauty and to the energies that underlay it.

At that point, the distinction between prose and poetry itself becomes insignificant, for, pushed to their limits, certain works of Surrealist criticism are barely distinguishable from poems. Whether art reviews, autobiographical accounts, or political broadsides, these texts—their style reflecting the jagged sonorities of Lautréamont's *Maldoror,* the syncopated syntax of Jacques Vaché's letters (on which, more later), and the jump-cut aesthetics of cinema—eschew objective pronouncements and relate more directly to the personalized viewpoints of critics like Hunter S. Thompson, Joan Didion, or Tom Wolfe, which they anticipated by several decades. Here, for example, is an excerpt from René Crevel's essay on "The Patriotism of the Unconscious":

> Everything will turn out fine, the show will all end with a song, as long as good old bawdiness rules the roost. And she understands the art of using up leftovers. If it has to do with the sexual instinct, quickly, she is expert in it, the smarty pants, she's in the know and, with a salacious smile, she spices up the scraps, carcasses, and giblets that have been sucked and sucked again from the reactionary old nanny goat.[33]

Less static, less authoritarian, less laboriously *reasoned* than what we traditionally think of as criticism, especially academic criticism, such renegade approaches, however resistant to definition and sober analysis, however dependent on a line of thinking that is (to use Breton's terminology) serpentine rather than linear—or rather, because of all this—might well lead us to a closer understanding of what Surrealism had, and has, to tell us.*

Among the most striking transformations of critical thinking, in both concept and expression, is Salvador Dalí's theory of paranoia-criticism. Related to the centuries-old tradition of the *image-devinette* or *image d'Epinal,* from Arcimboldo's vegetal

*I'm well aware that the present book is written in precisely the style the Surrealists were rebelling against. To experience the kind of criticism they were inventing, the reader might simply skip directly to their writings.

faces to Wittgenstein's duck-rabbit to the ubiquitous dual image of "What's on a man's mind" (a naked woman reclining or Sigmund Freud's profile), paranoia-criticism superimposes two realities to bring out a third. Dalí defined it as "a spontaneous method of *irrational knowledge* based on the critical and systematic objectification of delirious associations and interpretations."[34] His inspiration, he claimed, came from seeing what appeared to be a face by Picasso, which when restored to the horizontal position turned out to be an ethnographic photo of African tribesmen in front of a hut. From this, and from his readings of the psychoanalyst Jacques Lacan, he deduced that a similar mental process would allow two objects to coexist in the same image, bringing forth realities latent in each; as he noted, "paranoid delirium already constitutes in itself a form of interpretation."[35] Many of Dalí's canvases—which he called "hand-painted color photographs of concrete irrationality"—such as *Invisible Sleeping Woman Horse Lion* (1930) and *Metamorphosis of Narcissus* (1937), forefront these interpretations and interpenetrations. But no doubt the purest visual and verbal expression of paranoia-criticism is his 1963 study on "the tragic myth of Millet's *Angelus.*" In prose that mutates from straight-faced exegesis to wild fabulation to self-referential divagation, Dalí demonstrates how Millet's iconic canvas—at once "insipid and imbecilic" and "the most troubling, the most enigmatic, the densest, the richest in unconscious thought that ever was"[36]—harbors the germ of everything from a praying mantis to a memento mori to an erotic cartoon to a coffee service.

Externalizing the process of paranoia-criticism, Dalí began creating "objects with symbolic functions," small assemblages meant to inspire (as the critic Maurice Nadeau wrote) "a violent and indefinable emotion, doubtless having some relations with unconscious sexual desires"—although the aim was not to satisfy such desires, but rather to elicit some form of "irritation, the kind provoked by the disturbing perception of a *lack*."[37] The rest of the group riffed on paranoia-criticism by developing their own "Surrealist objects," or objects that negated the notion of utility. These included exhibition staples like Meret Oppenheim's aptly named *Object* (1936; also known as *Fur-Lined Cup and Saucer* or *Breakfast in Fur*), Alberto Giacometti's *Suspended Ball* (1930–31), and Dalí's *Lobster Telephone* (1936), but also more artisanal and ephemeral assemblages by those who did not normally practice the plastic arts, and who now explored forms of nonverbal poetry that cared little for polish or technical virtuosity. René Crevel went straight for the erotic content of these creations in his essay on Dalí: "No more coverings on objects or condoms on ideas. Today, if objects get hard-ons, that's no metaphorical fancy. And they're not getting hard in solitude: they're feeling each other up, sucking each other off, penetrating each other—these Surrealist objects are making love!"[38]

There was also Breton's particular corollary, the poem-object, which could be seen either as assemblages of items (pipe, stone, butterfly) intermingled with text, or as "poems in which certain directly perceptible objects . . . meld into the words."[39] (Breton also created perhaps the earliest use of the comic-strip motif in art, a 1943 collage called *Tragic, in the Manner of the "Comics,"* anticipating a conceit that would become a staple of Pop Art two decades later.)

Spontaneous, made of disparate materials, easily destroyed, these objects were a means of externalizing the poetic energy sought in automatism and dreams. Produced mainly in the mid-1930s, they trace a direct line forward to Found Art, Appropriation Art, Cornell's boxes, and the creations of early Pop artists such as Robert Rauschenberg and Jasper Johns. The painter Eileen Agar considered these objects the quintessential Surrealist creation: "Nothing that the movement has produced is more authentic, more varied, more personal and at the same time so anonymous."[40] They also hark back to such pre-Surrealist manifestations as Duchamp's "assisted readymades"—most notably *Why Not Sneeze, Rrose Sélavy?* (1921), a birdcage filled with lumps of sugar that upon lifting turned out to be of much heavier marble—and Man Ray's *The Gift* (1921), a flatiron with a row of carpet tacks down the middle (about which one recent critic highlighted "its attack on domestic chores, and their hierarchies, in the name of unreason").[41] No doubt the most monumental such work, and an important Surrealist precursor, is Ferdinand Cheval's Ideal Palace (1879–1912), a fabulously uninhabitable structure that a provincial mailman assembled over three decades from stones on his path, inspired by a vision in his dreams, and that Breton extolled as a prime example of "concrete irrationality in architecture."[42]

Other objects were left virtually untouched, reimagined and

reenergized simply by virtue of context. The most famous examples include Duchamp's original readymades (urinal, snow shovel, bottle rack), which became works of art simply because he affixed his signature, as well as Picasso's *The Venus of Gas* (1945), a rusty iron burner from a gas stove that the artist divinified by standing it upright—from household salvage to the goddess of love in the flick of a wrist.

Situated outside both art and functionality, of categories of "high" and "low," Surrealist objects upend our conceptions of three-dimensional existence. Their makers considered them antiproducts, a defiance of capitalist commodification, ambiguous in their purpose and bewildering in their aspect. Given their egalitarian facture, Breton likened them to Lautréamont's motto about "poetry made by all." More than anything, however, he saw them as "a precipitate of our desire," crystallizations of the real functioning of thought, and "the objectification of the very act of dreaming, its transformation into reality."[43]

The key term here is desire, the "acute awareness" that Penelope Rosemont highlighted. Surrealism was a revolution of the mind but also of the emotions. Intense emotive states, whether provoked by sleep trances, chance discoveries, found objects, or the ecstasies of sex, are a disruptive force, and disruption demands new forms, or the recasting of old forms—an infusion of poetry in all aspects of language, visual, verbal, and gestural. A new form suggests a new way to experience the world. Receptiveness to desire and openness to marvels are communicating vessels, with the capacity to endlessly regenerate our ways of being and help us resist the mind-deadening realities that surround us, but also to transform those realities into something better. As with Jacques Hérold wandering through the "gray streets" of Paris, marvels spring from without and within. Surrealist wonder, that "feathery wind," is like a drug trip without narcotics or a religious state without theology—the Beyond in our time—if only we know not so much where to look as *how* to look.

3 appropriation:

love and theft

Since the age of Ecclesiastes, we've had it drummed into us that there is nothing new under the sun, that art is an amalgam of previous works, formed of the splinters lodged through exposure to others' expressions. Jonathan Lethem suggests as much when he writes (in prose that is itself pieced together from various sources) that literature "has always been a crucible in which familiar themes are continually recast. . . . The kernel, the soul—let us go further and say the substance, the bulk, the actual and valuable material of all human utterances—is plagiarism. For substantially all ideas are secondhand, consciously and unconsciously drawn from a million outside sources."[1] Among the unattributed sources Lethem is appropriating is the Surrealist hero Lautréamont, who under his birth name Isidore Ducasse wrote in 1870: "Plagiarism is necessary. Progress implies it. It closely grasps an author's sentence, uses his expressions, deletes a false idea, replaces it with the right one."[2] Lautréamont knew whereof he spoke: not only did he lard *Maldoror* with liftings from Romantic and picaresque literature (much as Breton and Soupault later did in *The Magnetic Fields*), but he fashioned much of his second book, *Poésies,* from retooled maxims by the great moralists—including the above-quoted one about plagiarism, which is virtually swiped from the eighteenth-century aphorist Vauvenargues. So is *Poésies* Lautréamont's book, or should it more properly be considered the work of Vauvenargues, Pascal, and La Rochefoucauld?

"Appropriation" is a complex word. On the one hand indicative of creative subversion and transformation, it also implies plundering from sources—artworks, communities, cultures—not your own, and perhaps off-limits to you. Much as early modernists like Van Gogh and Picasso had turned to non-European, especially African and Japanese, art for inspiration, so the Surrealists looked to the arts of Oceania and Native America for an aesthetic experience—and even more so, an *emotional* experience—that they often found lacking in mainstream European productions.[3] In these Indigenous works, the Surrealists recognized a quality of mystery and wonder that radiated beyond time and beyond culture.

But that recognition is itself complex. While not as blatantly as a Picasso or a Van Gogh, some Surrealist artists, such as Ernst (who occasionally donned Hopi dress after moving to New Mexico), Man Ray, Giacometti, and Matta incorporated elements from what were then called "primitive" cultures into their visual output, revitalizing their work and the viewer's experience but obscuring the identity of the original. Similarly, the Surrealist writers absorbed the arts and thinking of these cultures into what they saw as a shared vision: Breton, for instance, likened Inuit art to his concept of beauty "envisaged exclusively to produce passion" in poems such as "Full Margin" and "The States General." An assiduous collector of Oceanic statues, Inuit masks, and

Hopi Kachina dolls, he maintained that these objects "justify the Surrealist vision, and even give it a new impetus"; and he postulated "very deep affinities between so-called 'primitive' thought and Surrealist thought: both want to overthrow the hegemony of consciousness and daily life." (He might have added that the arts of Oceania, for instance, which are rooted not in individual creativity but in a collective dynamic, mirror the Surrealist ethos of group creation.)[4] Was he honoring a shared inspiration, co-opting the energies of others, or both?

There is a hegemonic impulse to the avant-garde, a tendency toward absorption and repurposing, whether Picasso smuggling African masks into his *Demoiselles d'Avignon* or Richard Prince recropping the Marlboro Man for *Untitled (cowboy)* (1989). Breton, for one, was not immune to annexing what he saw as others' sympathetic efforts into a kind of Greater Surrealism, especially when he feared, as he periodically did, that the movement was losing steam. Not to say that he was always successful at it: In the early 1930s, a ham-fisted attempt to bring the Surrealist-influenced collective Le Grand Jeu under his umbrella ended up costing him a number of his existing colleagues. And when Frida Kahlo learned that a gallery show of her work that Breton had organized was being presented under the banner of the Paris group (with which she felt scant affinity), her tart response was, "I never knew I was a Surrealist until André Breton came to Mexico and told me I was one. I myself still don't know what I am."[5] Hal Foster pertinently cautions that "for all Surrealism's political bona fides . . . colonialism was one of its conditions of possibility: many of the Oceanic objects that beguiled the [Parisian Surrealists] came from French colonies, and even the Surrealist map ["The World in the Time of the Surrealists"] is imperial in its carving up of the world."[6]

Still, if one approaches foreign elements not as a conqueror but as a pilgrim, in a spirit of reciprocity, the dialogues might conceivably be energizing and mutually enriching. Breton, in surrounding himself with Indigenous objects, was on the one hand practicing a form of colonialism, but he was also trying to enter into and understand the principle of these objects' energy. To use an old terminology, he wanted to be inspired by them and, I would argue, to inspire in return, just as the energy that the Latin American "Boom" novelists derived from Faulkner energized a subsequent generation of U.S. authors, or as modern Chinese poets took inspiration from Pound's Chinese-inspired *Cathay.* It's a delicate balance between dialogue and pilfering, often hampered by one's conditioned blinders, but sometimes enhanced by intuitive sympathy in a kind of cultural profit-sharing. Claude Lévi-Strauss, who sometimes accompanied Breton to the Paris flea market, recalled the Surrealist leader's recognition of intrinsic qualities in pieces that Lévi-Strauss himself, as a trained anthropologist, had dismissed as tourist junk: "Breton had an instinct about objects he loved, and he sometimes made me appreciate things I otherwise wouldn't have seen or appreciated."[7]

In deriving objects and ideas from these Indigenous works, the Surrealist artists were attempting to distill their qualities. Their aim was not to replicate the native artworks but rather to convey, in the visual language of their own time and place, what they understood as their essence, and through this to give something back—as evidenced by the many appropriations of Surrealism throughout the world, even into the present day. To emphasize these cross-pollinations, they often mixed Indigenous works with Surrealist works in their exhibitions, giving each equal weight, inviting visitors to view each kind of art with refreshed eyes. While their elevation of non-Western arts and artists can itself be hegemonic, and while their defense of these arts is at times "shaped by contemporary racial stereotypes,"[8] as one historian put it, their comparatively nonexoticizing approach, and their refusal of essentialist conventions, helped open a path to current reevaluations of Eurocentric hierarchies that had long gone unchallenged.

In this regard, the Surrealists' engagement with racial otherness offers an object lesson in fruitful cross-cultural borrowings, even as it surfaces a number of troubling ambiguities. Almost to a person (with the notable exception of the unapologetically racist Dalí), the Surrealists aligned themselves with people of color, attacking French colonialism and the abuses it fostered at home and abroad.

They were not unique in this, but neither were they in the mainstream. While the comparatively liberal atmosphere of Paris in the 1920s attracted Black Americans such as Josephine Baker and Charlie Parker, for instance, and while France had abolished slavery well before many of its neighbors (it was outlawed by the Revolution of 1789, reinstated by Napoleon in 1802, then definitively banned in 1848), the interwar years nonetheless were marked by numerous acts of racial violence. This was especially true against North Africans (as late as 1990, nearly 40 percent of French people polled admitted an "aversion" to Arabs),[9] but it in no way spared the country's Black, Asian, Romani, and, need it be said, Jewish populations.

In 1941, as a sign of solidarity against the collaborationist Vichy government of Philippe Pétain, Breton invited the Afro-Cuban-Chinese artist Wifredo Lam to illustrate his latest book, *Fata Morgana,* telling a journalist from the conservative *Le Figaro* that the choice of Lam was meant "to make clear just how sympathetic I am to Marshal Pétain's racist concepts." (To Breton's disgust, the newspaper omitted that particular quotation from the published interview.) Not long after, in Martinique, he met and collaborated with the poets Aimé and Suzanne Césaire, co-founders of the Négritude movement. And in 1945, while on a lecture tour in Haiti, Breton told a student audience that "the greatest impulses toward new paths for Surrealism have been furnished" by his "friends of color," Aimé Césaire and Wifredo Lam.[10]

"Surrealism is allied with people of color," Breton later declared, "because it has always been on their side against every form of white imperialism and banditry." When, several weeks after his lecture to the students, a popular uprising deposed the repressive, U.S.-backed Haitian president Elie Lescot, some pointed to Breton's statements as a catalyst. Breton himself claimed no role in the overthrow, telling an interviewer who gave him too much credit: "Let's not exaggerate. At the end of 1945, the poverty, and consequently the patience, of the Haitian people had reached a breaking point." But Roger Gaillard, who had attended the lecture, insisted that Breton's words had "helped create, beyond any doubt, a climate among young people of my generation, a confidence in ourselves and in the future." And the journalist and poet René Bélance added that while Breton "had no intention of disturbing the political order of a country which was not his own," the "banal fact was that to speak of liberty—at that moment—was certainly a subversive act."[11]

All well and good. But figures like Lam and the Césaires, as well as Hector Hippolyte, Hervé Télémaque, René Ménil, Léopold Senghor, Jules Monnerot, Pierre Yoyotte, Ted Joans, and Will Alexander, remain an oft-neglected minority among the many who have passed through Surrealism, and only recently have such artists and writers begun receiving serious attention from historians of the movement—though how much of this is due to basic Eurocentrism on the part of the powerful Paris group and how much to the ignorance or disregard of commentators is difficult to parse. Let's not forget that even the well-intentioned are prey to implicit bias: though invited by the Paris group to share in their activities, Wifredo Lam confessed that he felt like "an exotic creature, like an African or Oceanic sculpture from the Pacific."[12] Nor must we brush under the rug the ingrained prejudice evident in declarations by those who consider themselves antiracist, such as Breton's remark that he would sleep with "any non-white woman, as long as she wasn't a Negress." Asked why, he claimed "physical repugnance" and the risk of children, "which is always possible."[13]

A similar ambivalence is found on the cultural level. All the while promoting a broad internationalism, the Paris, Brussels, and London Surrealist groups kept their focus mainly on a predominately white, European set of references: this was their comfort zone, and this is what they knew. Still, this did not prevent them from taking a genuine interest in cultural manifestations outside of their frame of reference, or from promoting races and ethnicities not their own.

A case in point is the relationship of the movement to Judaism, with which the French Surrealists had little contact and about which they had little to say, even though some of its members—among them, Man Ray, Tristan Tzara, Simone Kahn Breton, Claude Cahun, Kurt Seligmann, Victor Brauner, Jacques Hérold, Joyce Mansour, and Nelly Kaplan—came from Jewish backgrounds. The Jewish American writer and translator Edouard Roditi, when asked whether Breton was anti-Semitic, said that it was more a question of limited horizons: "He came from a social background where he'd never had any contact with Jews." Nonetheless, when the rabid anti-Semite Louis-Ferdinand Céline came up for rehabilitation in the 1950s, the Surrealist group fired off a letter to the newspaper *L'Express,* furiously denouncing his "infamy and intellectual filth."[14]

Sometimes this promotion took a form that was mainly rhetorical, as with their call in a 1925 broadside for "the Mongols . . . to set up camp in our squares." But other texts demonstrate a more informed solidarity with populations that were subject to persecution and oppression, such as the aggressive opposition to French colonialism expressed in statements like Paul Eluard's "The Suppression of Slavery" (1925) and the collective "Don't Visit the Colonial Exhibition!" (1931), for which they organized a counterexhibition called "The Truth About the Colonies"; or Eluard's "Yen-Bay" (1930), which protested the execution of Vietnamese resisters to French occupation: "There are only two races in the world: the oppressors and the oppressed"[15]—sentiments later echoed in the 1947 tract "Freedom Is a Vietnamese Word," which preceded the rout at Dien Bien Phu by seven years. Another collective tract, "Murderous Humanitarianism" (1934), originally published in Nancy Cunard's *Negro: An Anthology*, denounced the "counterfeit liberalism" of "snivelling capitalism" that exploits while pretending betterment: "The white man preaches, doses, vaccinates, assassinates and (from himself) receives absolution. With his psalms, his speeches, his guarantees of liberty, equality and fraternity, he seeks to drown the noise of his machine-guns."[16] And in 1960, several Surrealists collaborated on the "Declaration Concerning the Right of Insubordination in the Algerian War" (more familiarly known as the "Declaration of the 121," after the number of initial signatories), which called for active resistance to French government policy in Algeria and supported the Algerian separatists.

In addition to the content, the tone and tenor of these protests inspired various groups outside of Europe to develop their own, independent brands of Surrealism, which assimilated aspects of the European movement but maintained significant differences. Two important expressions in particular, both of a specifically Black vision, show how Surrealist practices and attitudes could be co-opted to subvert not only colonial oppression and supremacist hierarchies but also the movement's own limitations.

In 1941, while en route to wartime refuge in the United States,

Breton spent several weeks in Martinique, where he discovered and made contact with the poet Aimé Césaire. Césaire had recently published his masterwork *Notebook of a Return to My Native Land* (1939), which excoriated white political and cultural dominion over the island with Maldororian accents:

> Get away, I said, you bastard of a cop, swine get away. I hate the livery of order and the fish-hooks of hope. Get away foul ju-ju, bedbug of a monk. Then I turned to dream for him and his lost ones' paradises more calm than the face of a woman telling lies.[17]

Breton later called it "the greatest lyrical monument of our times" and spent much of his stopover in Martinique in conversation with Césaire and the group around the dissident periodical *Tropiques,* which included Césaire's wife, Suzanne, and René Ménil. For his part, Césaire recalled his meeting with Breton as "utterly crucial and decisive," and explained: "Surrealism provided me what I had been confusingly searching for. I have accepted it joyfully because in it I have found more of a confirmation than a revelation." Because of Surrealism, Suzanne Césaire wrote, "voices that would not be what they are [without it] resound everywhere."[18]

The "liberating factor" of Surrealism, as Aimé Césaire put it, was a primary influence on the Négritude movement, partly through Breton's visit to Martinique and partly through the presence of Martinican Surrealists such as Pierre Yoyotte and Jules Monnerot.[19] Négritude—the term was intended as a provocative challenge to the French racial slur "*nègre*"—had been developed in the 1930s by Césaire, in concert with the Senegalese poet and future president Léopold Senghor, the French Guianese poet and diplomat Léon-Gontran Damas, and the Martinican writers and journalists Jane and Paulette Nardal. It began in response to the oppression that had long been inflicted on the African diaspora, and more generally as an examination of Black identity in a white-dominated world. Though originally centered on French colonialism and the Afro-French experience, it influenced in turn a number of liberation movements in Europe, the Caribbean, and the United States.

Surrealism was not the only constituent factor in Négritude, which also took much of its inspiration from the Harlem Renaissance, to which the Nardals had introduced the others. Nor did Négritude have much to do with such core French Surrealist activities as automatic writing and collective games, focusing instead on the movement's political and social critiques. Like Surrealism, however, Négritude is a wide-ranging concept, embracing Césaire's "decolonization of the mind," Senghor's affirmation of traditional African customs (principles that became a basis of his presidency), and Damas's radical rejection of whiteness and wider incorporation of all colonized races. And, as with Surrealism, there have been schisms within the movement: René Ménil, for instance, criticized Senghor for "flattening out" the humor and "inherent ambiguity of poetic meaning" in Césaire's writings, and for playing into institutionalized racism by characterizing the Black mind as essentially "intuitive" and emotional, in contrast to white "rationality."[20]

More than anything, Négritude displays its affiliation with Surrealism in the two movements' shared anticolonialism and anticapitalism, intrinsic spirit of revolt, battle for cultural legitimacy, blurred boundaries between high and popular culture, and subversion of prescribed linguistic usages. Discussing the movement in 1967, Aimé Césaire called Surrealism "a weapon that exploded the French language. It shook up absolutely everything." The poets of Négritude adapted Surrealist tenets to their use, drawing mainly on African rather than European sources, and accepting the movement, said Senghor, "as a means, but not as an end, as an ally, and not as a master." That said, the relationship remains a complex one, and Surrealism has not always avoided criticism from the heirs of Négritude, particularly the writers associated with Creolism (including the Goncourt laureate Patrick Chamoiseau). Responding to an attack on Césaire in 1993, the Surrealist writer Annie Le Brun was herself attacked by Chamoiseau and the Creolist author Raphaël Confiant as a white woman "motivated by the quivering of her ovaries" and with no right to speak on these matters.[21]

A more contemporary offshoot of Négritude, Afrosurrealism adopts the manifest illogicality of Surrealist productions "to expose this 'absurd' life that Black people lead, with extra emphasis on the weirdness, to emphasize just how surreal Black life can be," as a recent article describes it, citing books like Toni Morrison's *Beloved* (1987) and films like Jordan Peele's *Get Out* (2017).[22] D. Scot Miller, in his "Afrosurreal Manifesto" (2009), places the movement in the "RIGHT NOW," describing it as "the best description to the reactions, the genuflections, the twists, and the unexpected turns this 'browning' of White-Straight-Male-Western-Civilization has produced."[23] Miller references figures as diverse as Kara Walker, Kool Keith, Samuel R. Delany,

Kehinde Wiley, Yinka Shonibare, Nick Cave, Ishmael Reed, Romare Bearden, Wangechi Mutu, Sun Ra, and the Marvel superhero Black Panther as representative of the Afrosurrealist pantheon. Suzanne Césaire's credo about being "in permanent readiness for the marvelous" is a watchword, as well as a direct link back to European Surrealism's primary motivations. Where it leans more toward Négritude than toward its European predecessor is in its concentration on a specifically Black experience.[24]

Then again, as the artist and performance poet Ted Joans might point out, this could be a distinction without a difference. Joans, who became involved with Surrealism after a chance meeting with Breton at a bus stop in 1960, and who participated in the Paris group's activities until its dissolution in 1969, brought the perspectives of a Black American hipster to the Europeans, combining the poetry of Rimbaud, Jarry, and Breton with the jazz of Charlie Parker, Thelonious Monk, and Cecil Taylor, the writings of Frantz Fanon and W. E. B. Du Bois, the political rhetoric of Patrice Lumumba and Malcolm X, and his own experiences as a Black man in the Jim Crow South to forge a Surrealism that speaks to, as Penelope Rosemont put it, "the social needs of our time."[25] His attraction to Surrealism largely rested on its antiracist stances, which aligned with Joans's engagement with the Black Power and Pan-African movements. He maintained that Surrealism was in fact born in Africa and characterized Africa as "a Surrealist continent, thus the most marvelous."[26] Only now gaining true critical recognition, Joans illustrates how Surrealist subversion can be assimilated into ongoing struggles against racial and cultural inequities. As he once summed it up,

> We are not shadows of yesteryear's surrealists, although we have been nourished by "them and those," and their "this and that" can be found engrained in the very marrow of our bones. . . . Although André Breton is gone, his spirit is still contagious. . . . Surrealists are committed to the cause of total emancipation. . . . We have the power and that power's color is black.[27]

Taking the givens of the status quo and repurposing them is a time-honored tool of revolt. In this regard, one of the most notable examples is the Surrealists' appropriation of advertising techniques. When Breton, in an early letter to Aragon, remarked that "Christianity is an advertisement for heaven," he was being both metaphorical and literal: that is, both undermining the lofty ethereality claimed by the church and forcing us to reexamine the pervasiveness of publicity in all aspects of our lives. He later remarked that he'd wanted to compose "an advertisement for heaven" that would be "striking enough, convincing enough" to make everyone who saw it commit suicide.[28]

Advertising is about persuading, but first it's about attracting attention. It was Guillaume Apollinaire who had proclaimed surprise to be "*our greatest new resource,*"[29] and it was he who identified the element of surprise as most vital to the "new spirit." Under Dada, the future Surrealists learned a further refinement: not only how to shock audiences but how to make them sit up and take notice, and keep coming back for more. Today, we might call them influencers.

Since the beginning of his poetic adulthood, Breton had looked for ways to break language out of the cloister into which it had been shut by literary preciousness. Advertising, with its eagerness to appropriate linguistic conventions and twist them in search of effect, seemed a particularly fruitful means—one, moreover, that had more in common with high aesthetics than it would at first appear. "What is it that poetry and art do?" he wrote to Aragon. "They extol. Extolling is also the aim of advertising."[30] Like dream condensation or the surprise detours of automatic writing, the best advertisements reconfigure the familiar into something recognizable but different, renewing both language and its object in arresting new usages and compelling the viewer's awareness. As Aragon observed, "We said about a poem: would it stand up if we made it into a poster? would people in the street stop to read it?"[31] Among the poems that stopped me in my tracks when I read them years ago, and that strike me as perfect examples of how appropriation can turn the humdrum into the intriguing, are Breton's "PSTT," an unretouched transcript of the "Breton" listings in the Paris phone book, and Aragon's "Suicide," which reads in its entirety:

A b c d e f
g h i j k l
m n o p q r
s t u v w
x y z

Benefiting from Tzara's PR chops (Tzara, whose "Manifesto 1918" had proclaimed that "advertising and business are also poetic elements"),[32] the poets and provocateurs who made up the Surrealist group knew their way around the promotional terrain.

The movement's early works make frequent reference to the attention-grabbing artifacts of the modern world—billboards for Mazda light bulbs, at a time when electrification of the capital was still a recent phenomenon, and the soap shill Bébé Cadum (whom Robert Desnos cast as the epic hero of his novel *La Liberté ou l'amour*), shop mannequins, couture labels, signs on building façades, and other advertising flotsam—co-opting them, well before Pop Art came along, as purveyors of quotidian marvels, as well as catchy symbols. (The process came full circle as early as the 1930s, when advertising, that most capitalist of endeavors, began appropriating surrealistic imagery for its own purposes—as did that other haut-bourgeois manifestation, fashion design. Meanwhile, as is well known, Dalí, whom Breton snarkily nicknamed "Avida Dollars," decorated the windows of the Bonwit Teller department store and the covers of *Vogue* and *Town and Country,* contributed to movies by Hitchcock and Disney, drew the logo for Chupa Chups lollipops that is still in use today, devised motifs for fabrics, rugs, and neckties, endorsed products right and left, and energetically promoted his own brand.)[33]

Returning to Breton's *Manifesto of Surrealism,* it's worth underscoring that a manifesto is by nature an exercise in persuasion, in extolling. As noted earlier, it became the primary announcement for the nascent Surrealist movement, as well as a conclusive retort to Goll's and Dermée's rival claim. But wait, there's more! For the *Manifesto* was initially conceived not as the mission statement of a new movement, but as, indeed, a targeted advertisement. Breton was discouraged by the neglect that had greeted the publication of *The Magnetic Fields* in 1920, which, despite his high hopes for it and for automatic writing, had gone virtually unnoticed. Now preparing a new collection of automatic texts, to be called *Soluble Fish,* he decided to arm the volume with a short theoretical preface, an explanation of automatism that, this time around, would clue the reader in to its radical significance. Even as the preface eventually swelled into a full-fledged manifesto and overshadowed the product it was selling—or rather, ended up selling a different product—its promotional DNA remained intact.

In the *Manifesto,* Breton demonstrates a fundamental truth of both writing and advertising: that it is first and foremost a process of seduction. His illustrative anecdotes are related with consummate storytelling flair. His nicely encapsulated definitions of Surrealism, his lists of precursors, like sponsors or guarantors, and his "secret" recipes, like miracle solutions to life's quandaries, are so many catchy soundbites for readers (and reviewers) to latch onto. Breton is perfectly aware that surreality is heady stuff; and even though, like any good pitchman, he aims to put it "within everyone's reach,"[34] he also knows that his particular blend of tonic might be hard to swallow. To keep the reader engaged, he weaves a mystique around himself and his companions in the text, laying open his world like a proverbial book, giving the illusion of uniquely privileged access. His writings, in the *Manifesto* and elsewhere, are littered with mentions of his friends of the moment, cited with an authority and an assurance that confer on a bunch of young unknowns a virtual fame (which, in a process not unfamiliar to anyone with an online following, then became actual fame). These are not simply in-jokes: by refusing to draw a distinction between private and public facts, Breton endows this ragtag band of fellow travelers with mythic life, daring us to ignore them.

Despite limited financial and technological resources, the Surrealists cannily used the means at their disposal to broadcast their message and make it stick. Surrealism was born into a world of paper and ink, of radio waves and the comparatively new medium of celluloid images. We can only imagine what the group would have done with the instant worldwide messaging and creative possibilities afforded by smartphones and streaming video, by Photoshop and Snapchat and Instagram and TikTok—all the more so in that, as the historian Georges Sebbag has pointed out, many of the techniques the early Surrealists used anticipated current media practices, such as inviting readers directly into the text by mentioning "here and now" details of the time or place in which it was being written.[35]

They were savvy about branding, remaining vigilant about Surrealist methods or productions being counterfeited, and vigorously opposing any "Surrealist exhibition" (notably the two major MoMA shows in 1936 and 1968) that didn't get their imprimatur. They applied the company label to their public manifestations, launching a Surrealist Editions publishing imprint, a Bureau of Surrealist Research study center, a *Surrealist Revolution* magazine (succeeded over time by *Surrealism in the Service of the Revolution,* an *International Bulletin of Surrealism* in several languages, *Arsenal: Surrealist Subversion, Surrealism, Even,* and *Surrealist Junction*—and that's just the French group), numerous

International Exhibitions of Surrealism (along with more focused shows with titles like "First Papers of Surrealism" and "Surrealist Intrusion in the Enchanters' Domain"), and rarely let the epithet out of their watchful sight.

They took a multivalent strategy, combining readings with film showings, art exhibits with street demonstrations (in a through-line from Dada to Situationism to the Beats to the Happenings to guerrilla performance). They intervened in others' periodicals, and were not shy about making their viewpoint vehemently felt when protesting an event, political situation, or personal slight. When immediate action was required, these masters of anti-social media issued tracts and broadsides, distributed by various means—including, on one memorable occasion, by slipping a particularly offensive handout under the plates at a stodgy literary banquet and sparking a legendary brawl, turning the banquet into a de facto performance piece replete with fisticuffs, smashed mirrors, and swinging from the chandelier.

Today, many of their techniques might seem like standard procedure. But returning to Sebbag's comment about Surrealist intrusion in the advertisers' domain, it's worth remembering how new those practices were at the time; the fact that much of it now seems old hat is itself a measure of its influence over the past decades. Never mind the self-promoting antics of a Jeff Koons or Damien Hirst ("artist and entrepreneur," as Wikipedia defines the latter): artists have always been masterful at pushing themselves forward. But how much do Keith Haring or Banksy owe to the Surrealist desire to put art in the street? How far back can we go from street poetry, hip-hop, or slams before bumping into Aragon's question about the poem surviving as a poster? In the museum and gallery worlds, even today's more innovative exhibits feel like they haven't caught up with Surrealist strategies: the coal sacks that loomed over visitors at the 1938 International Exhibition, the twine that ensnared them in the 1942 "First Papers" show, the random lighting and abrupt darkness (to the roar of an oncoming train) that jolted them at Peggy Guggenheim's Art of This Century in the 1940s, in a gallery designed by Surrealist architect Frederick Kiesler. And Banksy might never have set *Girl with Balloon* (destroyed 2018) on auto-shred had Picabia not made a chalk drawing at a Dada show a century earlier, then had Breton sponge it away onstage.

That said, perhaps not every Surrealist innovation needs to be carried forward. In 1920 Breton and Soupault planned to conclude their self-performed play *If You Please* with an actual onstage suicide (they didn't). Four decades later, the Canadian conceptual artist Jean Benoît, under the auspices of the Surrealist group, performed a piece called *The Execution of the Testament of the Marquis de Sade.* Before an invited audience of one hundred writers and artists, Benoît appeared, dressed in a black costume with sharp protrusions over his chest and legs, a grotesquely extended erection, and a cape from which blood seemed to be dripping. Gradually his costume was removed by his wife, the artist Mimi Parent, revealing his nude body painted all in black, his heart covered by a red star: Sade's emblem. With a shrill cry, he seized a red-hot iron placed nearby and branded the word "Sade" into his flesh, squarely over his heart. He then held out the still-smoking iron to his audience and demanded, "Who's next?" The painter Roberto Matta was so carried away by the performance that he spontaneously rushed up, tore open his shirt, and seared his own left breast.[36] Breton's "advertisement for heaven," brought to you by a sponsor from hell.

4

subversion: identity paradigms

"Poetry," Breton said in 1922, "which is all I have ever appreciated in literature, emanates more from the lives of human beings—whether writers or not—than from what they have written or from what we might imagine they could write."[1] This peremptory assertion, which situated poetry not as Coleridge's "best words in the best order" but as a living attitude, was an early version of what in the 1960s was expressed as "the personal is political," and it implicated the poet or artist in the work created. It wasn't enough for you or your art to say the right things; if you were going to help solve "the principal problems of life," as the *Manifesto* put it, you also had to walk the walk.

Such declarations threaten to sound like one more of those windy pronouncements blowing through the capacious hallways of the avant-garde. For the Surrealists, however, the symbiosis between one's moral and aesthetic worth was a cornerstone of their worldview. A person's life was their most important "opus," and trumped any other production; otherwise put, a scum with a beautiful prose style was still a scum (*vide* the evergreen debates about Ezra Pound and Céline), while someone like Breton's friend Jacques Vaché, who barely wrote at all, could zoom to the top of the Surrealist pantheon on the strength of his actions and attitude alone. Recent controversies surrounding artists such as Chuck Close, Balthus, and everyone's favorite misogynist, Picasso, as well as such once-beloved performers as Woody Allen, Bill Cosby, Kevin Spacey, and Louis C.K., suggest both the complexity and the prescience of Breton's criterion.

Collectively and severally, the Surrealists rarely hesitated to express their likes and dislikes, and many of their choices were based more on ethical and moral considerations than on aesthetic ones. Breton began his *Second Manifesto* in 1929 by declaring, "More than anything else, Surrealism attempted to provoke, from the intellectual and moral point of view, *an attack of conscience,* of the most general and serious kind, and . . . the extent to which this was or was not accomplished alone can determine its historical success or failure." The historian Gérard Durozoi advances that Surrealism is in fact "the only movement of the twentieth century to espouse an ethic."[2]

The group's attempts to provoke this attack of conscience—what some would now call their forays into "cancel culture"—took a variety of forms, from published boycotts to live events. Among the latter, an early example, predating Surrealism itself, was the "Trial of Maurice Barrès." A renowned novelist, Barrès had been admired by Breton, Aragon, and other future Surrealists in their formative years as an exemplar of personal freedom, the so-called Prince of Youth, but with World War I he had hardened into a superpatriot and archconservative. Feeling betrayed, Breton and his friends staged a mock trial of Barrès in May 1921 before a packed house at the Hôtel des Sociétés Savantes, a handsome late-nineteenth-century edifice on the aptly named Rue

Danton in Paris's 6th arrondissement; the charge: "conspiracy against the security of the Mind." When the "court" ultimately handed down a sentence of twenty years' hard labor for Barrès, Breton, who had pushed for the death penalty, was disappointed. Barrès himself, of course, was nowhere near the proceedings and probably couldn't have cared less—this was, after all, before social media—but Breton had pursued his case with such ferocity that some wondered what might have happened had the novelist been present.[3]

Much less symbolic were the "excommunications" from within the Surrealists' own ranks. Beginning not long after the movement's founding and recurring periodically over the forty-five years of the Paris group's existence, these purges targeted members both prominent and minor, for failings that ranged from practicing hack journalism to not embracing the group's turn toward Communist politics (or, conversely, for not endorsing the group's later condemnation of Stalinist abuses, prosecuted with a fervor that would have made Stalin proud) to not condemning vehemently enough those whom the others had condemned. The excommunications were in part a referendum on loyalty—are you with the program or not?—and sometimes merely an outlet for personal spite, but more fundamentally they were an interrogation of identity: you are defined by the company you keep, and tolerating intolerable elements reflects back on you. If poetry emanates from life, what is needed for the life to live up to the demands of the poetry? And how well did the Surrealists live up to them?

Among the most urgent of these demands was provocation

as a spur to change: it's worth underscoring that the Surrealists, like Dada before them (though arguably with more constructive intent), were out to shock. Whether in the aggressive prose and propositions of Breton's *Manifesto,* the group's overtures to the much reviled Communist Party, or broadsides like the Anatole France–trolling *A Corpse* ("To bury his corpse, let someone on the quays empty out a box of those old books 'he loved so much' and put him in it and throw the whole thing into the Seine," went a typical statement) and the "Open Letter to Mr. Paul Claudel, French Ambassador to Japan" ("We profoundly hope that revolutions, wars, and colonial insurrections will annihilate this Western civilization whose vermin you defend even in the Orient"),[4] their actions were not only steps toward defining a philosophical program but also ways of slapping bourgeois proprieties repeatedly across the face.

As such, the Surrealists issued a number of statements condemning virtually every fundamental that French society held dear. They spat on formal education, addressing a vehement denunciation of the pedagogical system "to the Rectors of European Universities" (which begs the irony that our knowledge of Surrealism today is largely maintained by university courses and scholarly studies). They demanded that prison doors be unlocked and the army disbanded ("Nothing, neither the recognition of a committed crime nor contribution to the national defense, can force man to give up his freedom").[5] They celebrated crime, not only the fictional gratuitous killing committed by André Gide's character Lafcadio in *Les Caves du Vatican* (1914; known in English as *Lafcadio's Adventures*) but also real-life murders by Violette

Nozières, Germaine Berton, and the Papin sisters; the fact that these women had killed tainted authority figures—abusive father, right-wing journalist, employers—gave the Surrealists' support a transgressive cast, even if partially diluted by its sexualized nature. Robert Desnos called for a new Terror, on the model of the French Revolution. Breton asserted that "Surrealism was not afraid to make for itself a tenet of total revolt, complete insubordination, of sabotage according to rule . . . [expecting] nothing save from violence," and, in one of the movement's most notorious statements, defined the "simplest Surrealist act" as "dashing down into the street, pistol in hand, and firing blindly, as fast as you can pull the trigger, into the crowd"[6]—a statement that he came to regret after the mechanized slaughter of World War II, and that the current rise in gun violence and mass shootings marks with a permanent stain.

"One of the key strategies in a Surrealist mode of inquiry," writes a recent commentator, "is to seek the tabooed, to find out what it is we're not allowed to say or to know."[7] It was in this spirit that the Surrealists openly embraced blacklisted figures as role models, most glaringly the Marquis de Sade: Breton featured Sade in his *Anthology of Black Humor;* Buñuel gave his sociopathic hero the Duc de Blangis a pivotal role in *L'Age d'or;* Man Ray, Eluard, and Desnos enshrined him in image and verse. In part it was the outrageously stylized acts of degradation Sade depicts that engaged the Surrealists' sense of iconoclasm, while his brief and heated membership in the Revolutionary government appealed to hotheads like Aragon, who had adopted Saint-Just's dictum, "No freedom for the enemies of freedom." But the real attraction lay in Sade's challenge to bourgeois morals, for alongside the black humor of his descriptions, he wrote many pages of philosophical disquisition that sketch an unsparing and unsentimental vision of human ethics, and strip away the pieties with which we have comforted ourselves for two millennia. "Sade wished to give back to civilized man the force of his primitive instincts," Eluard wrote. "He believed that in this way, and only in this way, would true equality be born. Since virtue is its own reward, he strove, in the name of all suffering, to abase and humiliate it . . . with no illusions and no lies, so that it might help all those it incites to build a world befitting man's immense stature." Or, as Sade himself put in the mouth of one of his fictional stand-ins in *Philosophy in the Bedroom* (1795): "Let us feel when it is to [our] advantage; and when it is not, let us be absolutely unbending. From this exact economy of feeling, from this judicious use of sensibility, there results a kind of cruelty which is sometimes not without its delights."[8] Coming well before Freud, Sade's unseasonably cold, resolutely materialist philosophy, in or out of the bedroom, upends our complacent belief in the basic goodness of people and forces us to observe human nature at its ugliest and most unnerving—thereby highlighting the questions that foment any meaningful revision of our interactions.*

*This does not obviate protests such as those by Andrea Dworkin, who warned that Sade's books, like any form of pornography, could incite acts of violence, especially against women—a charge lent credence by Matta's spontaneous self-broiling at Jean Benoît's *Testament* performance. But it does set Sade's writings in a different light from the one that casts him as merely a poster boy for aberrant sexuality.

With Sade's internment in Charenton Asylum no doubt in mind, the Surrealists attacked the psychiatric profession: an open letter "To the Head Doctors of Insane Asylums" repudiated any attempt to limit "the free development of a delirium." Breton the former psychiatric intern declared: "All confinements are arbitrary. . . . I know that if I were mad, after several days of confinement I should take advantage of any lapses in my madness to murder anyone, preferably a doctor, who came near me." Dalí wrote a "Declaration of the Independence of the Imagination and the Rights of Man to His Own Madness," in which he proclaimed "that all men are equal in their madness and that madness . . . constitutes the common base of the human spirit."[9] Beneath the aggressive postures, the Surrealists were demonstrating a compassion for the mentally ill and neurodiverse uncommon in their day, and that long predates the "anti-psychiatric" writings of R. D. Laing and David Cooper. And they were decades ahead of Michel Foucault in criticizing the normative and repressive aspects of psychiatry as it was, and often still is, practiced.

Perhaps most violently, the Surrealists took aim at religion, especially the Catholicism long dominant in France. Their collective "Address to the Pope," Péret's stridently anticlerical poems (not to mention the photo of him hurling invective at a clergyman that the group featured on the cover of *La Révolution surréaliste*), and their welcoming of the libertine defrocked priest Ernest Gengenbach were so many jabs at what Péret dubbed "the greatest spiritual and material obstacle to Western man's liberation."[10] Though some might object that the church no longer wields the same authority over society as it once did, the many fundamentalisms still prevalent throughout the world, not least of them the politically influential Christian conservative movement, would argue that the Surrealists' critiques of rigid religious dogmas have lost none of their urgency. And, as evidenced by works such as Banksy's *Cardinal Sin* (2011) and Trina McKillen's installation *Confess* (2019), both motivated by the Catholic Church's sex abuse scandals, there is still more to say.

The Surrealists denied the value of work, which takes on particular resonance in the vast reevaluation of labor dynamics following the lockdowns and closures of 2020–22 and such trends as the Great Resignation and quiet quitting. Few in the group held steady jobs; those who did were pressured to leave them, often at the cost of enduring precarious living conditions. Proponents of "noisy quitting," they blared "WAR ON WORK" on the cover of *La Révolution surréaliste;* Aragon blasted "bankers, students, workers, civil servants, domestics" as "the cocksuckers of the useful, the jerkoffs of necessity. I will never work. My hands are pure"; while the writer and activist André Thirion (Surrealist, member of the French Communist Party, and future Gaullist minister) shouted down such values as labor and money, arguing that the Party's glorification of work was itself anti-Communist: "I say shit on all those counterrevolutionaries and their miserable idol, WORK!"[11] Breton called for a strike of writers analogous to those of factory workers, and even at the height of the Surrealists' attempted rapprochement with the Communist Party was declaring his nonbelief in the utility of labor: "The event from which each of us is entitled to expect the revelation of his own life's meaning—that event which I may not yet have found, but on whose path I seek myself—*is not earned by work.*"[12] This was not simply a protest against the scandalously poor working conditions of French laborers, though the Surrealists condemned specific instances of that as well. More generally, it was a call to abolish the salary structure altogether, and all the societal evils that went with it. Among these, how could you remain available to the self-actualizations afforded by marvelous chance if you were stuck in a workaday existence? As Abigail Susik notes, the Surrealists "were anti-capitalists who, ahead of their time, imagined a post-work world. . . . It wasn't the activity of creative work as such that [they] decried [but rather] capitalism's system of wage earning as a means of survival."[13]

As impecunious poets and painters, the Surrealists weren't, of course, always able to avoid paid employment: distress oblige. Péret, Aragon, and Soupault occasionally worked as newspaper columnists or book editors, and Desnos hosted a radio program. Over the years, Breton held short-term gigs as Proust's reluctant proofreader (for which he was not gifted), a gallerist (ditto), a wartime radio announcer for the Voice of America, and an editor-at-large for the Gallimard publishing house; and he and Aragon served in their youth as curators to the wealthy couturier and collector Jacques Doucet (it was Breton who persuaded Doucet to buy Picasso's *Demoiselles d'Avignon,* which hung for years in the dressmaker's bathroom). Several of them also accepted subsidies from well-heeled benefactors such as the viscount Charles de Noailles, who underwrote books, periodicals, films, and travels. Still, many were the times when even dire necessity wasn't enough to make them bow to jobs or handouts, even if it meant living without electricity, heat, or adequate food.

While taken together this sounds like a heavily negative program—No to religious strictures! No to the rote conformity of the classroom! No to the drudgery of shop floor or office!—what lay behind it was much more aspirational. By highlighting and challenging the assumed paradigms of European civilization, the Surrealists meant to break humanity out of its complacent limitations and establish "freedom the color of man."[14]

On the one hand, we might wonder whether this has led anywhere: children still go to school, adults still go to work, and plenty of people still go to worship, asylums, or jail. But the discourse has changed in the past hundred years, and the nature of many of these institutions has undergone significant revision since the Surrealists made their pronouncements. Many social and historical factors have of course played into these revisions; but, as Susik suggests about work, in picking apart the complex debates that spurred them along, we will inevitably come across strands of the Surrealists' vehement protests, both as harbingers and as guideposts for further change.

Humor is a many-barbed thing. Among other functions, it coopts the forms and stances of that which holds itself most dear, turning these shibboleths bottom-up to expose their absurdity. It acts as a safeguard against oppressive power, regardless of whether this power is wielded by the self-serving or the self-righteous. Like Dadaist humor before it, Surrealist humor is a particularly corrosive form of subversion, the great guffaw that sticks a pin in fanaticism and zealotry, a middle finger to the self-serious posturing that massacres others or that flattens effervescence under the weight of dreary exegesis. Dictatorships, on the state or grassroots level, have no sense of it. As the Yugoslav Surrealist Koča Popević once put it, "Humor would be anarchy if it could be an attitude."[15]

In the 1930s, Breton codified the particularly Surrealist brand of humor—which he labeled black humor (*humour noir*), and which we'd now call dark humor—as a partly macabre, often nonsensical, wholly vitriolic turn of spirit that he termed "the mortal enemy of sentimentality" and "a superior revolt of the mind."[16] Its descendants include, among many others, the Theatre of the Absurd; the writings of Kurt Vonnegut, John Barth, et al.; television fare like *Monty Python's Flying Circus, Saturday Night Live,* and their avatars; the films of David Lynch, Guy Maddin, Alejandro Jodorowsky, and the Coen brothers; and cartoon characters like Bugs Bunny and virtually anything by Tex Avery.

Twisting our gaze backward, the precursors most often cited include Swift (whom Breton considered its "true initiator"), Duchamp, Jarry, Baudelaire, Poe, and Carroll. But no doubt the most influential name is one far less familiar than any of these: Jacques Vaché. A reluctant soldier of the Great War, Vaché met Breton by pure happenstance in 1916, while he was being treated for a leg wound in the ward where Breton was serving as a medical orderly. His impact on Surrealism would be profound, as shown not only in the essays Breton wrote over several decades about their brief friendship but also in the jagged, aggressive turns of many Surrealists' prose, which echo the staccato, acidic rhythms of Vaché's wartime letters, and more generally in the group's irreverent attitudes. "The enthusiasms — (in the first place they're noisy) — *of others* are abhorrent," Vaché wrote to Breton in 1917; and the following year: "— ART doesn't exist, no doubt — It is therefore useless to sing of it — and yet! people make art — because that's how it is and not otherwise — Well — what can you do — ? —"[17] "In Vaché's person, in utmost secrecy, a principle of total insubordination was undermining the world," Breton rhapsodized years later, "reducing everything that then seemed all-important to a petty scale, desecrating everything in its path."[18] It was Vaché—who as a recalcitrant warrior practiced what Breton termed "desertion within oneself," who sported a hybrid uniform of his own tailoring that was half-Allied and half-German, and who claimed he didn't mind dying but "object[ed] to being killed in wartime" (he in fact died, of a drug overdose that was or wasn't accidental, practically the minute the war ended)—who supplied the Ur-definition of humor as the Surrealists conceived it: "I believe it is a sensation — I almost said a SENSE — that too — of the theatrical (and joyless) pointlessness of everything."[19] The fact that we can now associate this "theatrical (and joyless) pointlessness" with comedy and not bat an eye shows how far into the Surrealist domain of humor we've traveled in a hundred years.

In trying to define Surrealist humor, it might be easier to begin with what it is not. Surrealist humor is not lighthearted, not well-meaning, not jovial or festive. It does not encourage fellowship or community but rather appropriates and subverts the techniques of hilarity to throw alienation in your face. It is antisocial and volatile, like a Molotov cocktail. Breton characterized it as "offensive, wholly new, absolutely savage," and he liked to recount how he and Vaché, when on leave, would go into a movie theater, set out food and wine, and enjoy a boisterous picnic while the film ran and the audience gaped at them. "I have never experienced anything quite as *magnetizing,*" he wrote. "The important thing is that we came out of it 'charged' for a few days."[20] (We think of Robert Louis Stevenson's game "Jink," involving "the most absurd acts for the sake of their own absurdity." We also think of shows like *Punk'd.*)

More than mere pranks, these flashes of humor (or "umor," as Vaché styled it) also served a more sober function, as a challenge to the rigid conventions fostered by so-called serious, adult society. In the *Manifesto,* Breton cites the wonder that children experience as a kind of lost paradise: "The mind which plunges into Surrealism relives with glowing excitement the best part of its childhood."[21] (Brancusi: "When we are no longer children we are already dead." Dylan: "He not busy being born is busy dying." Et cetera.) Children do not feel bound by adult laws of physics or behavior; they easily move in and out of roles and identities, assume the traits and trappings of others without a second thought. Barely out of childhood themselves, the early Surrealists sought to recapture that glowing excitement, sometimes by exploring hidden corners of the city and of their own psyches, and often by playing games. The irony is that, biographically speaking, many of the individuals attracted to Surrealism throughout its history had survived unhappy childhoods and conflictual relations with their parents, and were perhaps seeking in the movement and its community—and in Breton's authority as "anti-father"—a second chance at the paradise they'd never had an opportunity to lose.

Among Surrealist games, no doubt the best known is Exquisite Corpse (*cadavre exquis*), which involves composing a sentence in collaboration with several others, no one having seen what was already written. Developed soon after the movement's launch, the activity took its name from the first sentence produced: "The exquisite / corpse / shall drink / the new / wine." The verbal Exquisite Corpse evolved over time into various iterations, of which the most famous is its visual spinoff, in which the participants add the continuation of a hidden partial drawing or collage on a folded sheet of paper to create a composite, unplanned image (including the more contemporary examples described in Chapter 1). Like the verbal composites, the visual creations involved the entire group, artists and writers alike, whose talents joined indistinguishably.

Other frequently played games included Truth or Consequences, a "destroyer of fragile friendships" that required players to answer even the most uncomfortable questions with absolute honesty (seventy years later, Madonna refreshed and monetized the activity in the film *Truth or Dare*); and One Inside Another, an exercise in poetic analogy that involved describing one object in terms of a second (for example, a lion described as flame from a match), based on the idea that "any object is 'contained' within any other." There was also the Marseilles Game that a number of displaced Surrealists created in 1941, while waiting for uncertain passage out of France. Based on traditional playing cards, the Surrealist deck appropriated the standard motifs, transforming them into emblems of desire and resistance by replacing the four existing suits with Love, Dream, Revolution, and Knowledge, and the face cards with privileged figures from the Surrealist canon. Overall, Surrealist games were prized as a spur to creative thinking and intellectual honesty; and, as with automatic writing, their collective nature constituted a primary appeal.[22]

The importance Breton attached to such activities, and the level of commitment he expected from those present, struck some as excessive, especially those who saw them as parlor entertainment. But despite their emphasis on imagination and fancy, these games had an underlying gravity: their goal was revelation, not relaxation. Simone Breton recalled that André saw Exquisite Corpse, for instance, as "one of those natural sources or cascades of inspiration that he so loved discovering. The suggestive power of those arbitrary juxtapositions of words was so stupefying and dazzling, so brilliantly verified the Surrealist thesis and mentality, that the game became a system, a research method . . . perhaps even a drug."[23] Aragon, echoing Simone's earlier description of the sleeping fits, was struck by the "havoc" and "tang of disaster" that hovered over "these supposedly innocent occupations," the "kind of stupor that follows such games." And Claude Lévi-Strauss, who frequented the Surrealists in the 1940s, likened the games to an "initiation rite," calling to mind Johan Huizinga's contemporaneous observation that "formally speaking, there is no distinction whatever between marking out a space for a sacred purpose and marking it out for purposes of sheer play."[24]

Given the crisis atmosphere that often surrounded these games, particularly during the Nazi Occupation, when hosting them was grounds for arrest and execution, the mere fact of play was deadly serious; as one scholar notes, collective laughter in that context "was a subversive act, and irony and black humor were used for dissident ends." The Surrealist writer Jean-Louis Bédouin summed up such activities as "an effective measure against the temptation to sink into despair." And he specifies: "It was not a matter of trying to deny the gravity of the situation. It was a matter of preserving, at any cost, sufficient freedom of mind with respect to it."[25]

5 transgression:

free unions

"As soon as Surrealist methods begin to enjoy widespread favor," Breton predicted, "a new morality will have to be substituted for the prevailing morality, the source of all our trials and tribulations."[1] A cornerstone of this new morality was Eros, particularly the transgressive power that uninhibited eroticism might wield over restrictive societal norms. Giving our erotic impulses free rein was deemed nothing less than revolutionary. Péret, who termed the melding of profound emotion and elevated sexuality "sublime love," saw it as humanity's best means of revolt against religion and society. And Breton, who used the term "mad love," countered the prevailing Christian hierarchy of body and spirit by declaring carnal love and spiritual love to be coequals: "Here Surrealism deliberately departs from most traditional doctrines, which hold that carnal love is a mirage and passionate love a deplorable intoxication."[2] But as is often the case when it comes to sex, the movement's statements and actions betrayed a large share of ambivalence.

While Surrealism, in the popular imagination, enjoys a reputation for continuous licentiousness, all orgies all the time, the reality is that the young men who initially defined it were both quite serious about sexuality and sometimes even prudish. Georges Sebbag points out that, despite their veneration for Sade, despite novels like Aragon's *Irene's Cunt* and the X-rated verses of Aragon and Péret's *1929,* "they had much more in common with great romantics like Shelley, Nerval, and Achim von Arnim than with libertines and pornographers."[3] They abhorred marriage as an institution, but many of them were married, even if sometimes loosely. They promoted the idea that a grand passion could excuse any behavior, though this in itself became such a stricture that the "grand passion" in question was often an invented alibi. They celebrated "free union," as Breton titled one of his poems, and the power of the Freudian pleasure principle (Freud's seminal essay "The Ego and the Id" first appeared in French in 1927), and Rimbaud's famous dictum that "love has to be reinvented," but their conception of it was still essentially monogamous, built on the notion of an exclusive heterosexual couple rather than on more freely defined unions.

Not just simple lifestyle choices, these were criteria for acceptance or rejection. Discussing his preference for "passional and exclusive" love over polyamory, Breton later reflected that "the majority of quarrels that cropped up in Surrealism" were rooted in "an irreducible disagreement" over sexual matters.[4] Breton himself, caught between his liberal ideals, his personal insecurities, and his courtly belief in love as sacred and initiatory, tolerated these variations with discomfort—when he tolerated them at all. In many ways, the story of his relations with sexuality is the story of a man struggling with his own inhibitions, championing women's autonomy and equality in theory but having a hard time with it in practice, and the same could be said of others in the group.

In an attempt to move beyond the puritanism of their society and their upbringing, the Surrealists held twelve "inquiries on sexuality," beginning in 1928, in which they debated everything from masturbation to sex toys to threesomes to exhibitionism. The sessions were remarkably frank for the time, but they also highlighted how subject many of these avant-gardists were to old prejudices. Breton in particular expressed his dislike of, among other things, brothels ("places where everything has a price"), promiscuity, multiple partners, zoophilia, women's orgasms ("If I desire a woman, it makes no difference to me whether she comes or not"), sex with a woman you didn't love, pregnant women, and women who didn't speak French. Predictably, most of these sessions were among men only and reflected a uniquely male viewpoint. In practically the only session that a woman did attend, Youki Foujita, who would later marry Robert Desnos, listened for a while, then remarked, "You boys need to learn a few things."[5]

Still, despite their shortcomings, the discussions on sexuality show a sincere—if inadvertently revelatory—attempt to probe an issue most often repressed, at a time when even serious researchers were dismissing it (Freud, Krafft-Ebing, and Wilhelm Reich being the notable exceptions), and when novels such as D. H. Lawrence's *Lady Chatterley's Lover* and James Joyce's *Ulysses* were subject to prosecution. The fact that the first two of these conversations were rushed into print in *La Révolution surréaliste,* more or less unedited and uncensored, speaks to a certain urgency and desire for authenticity.

As Breton's remark about "irreducible disagreement" indicates, moreover, there was hardly unanimity in the group about sexual matters. While Breton championed serial monogamy and condemned male homosexuality—"I accuse homosexuals of confronting human tolerance with a mental and moral deficiency,"[6] he declared in the inquiries on sex—others were less blinkered. Queneau, Prévert, and Tanguy defended love between two men, provoking Breton's and Péret's ire. René Crevel openly defended and wrote about his bisexuality. Claude Cahun, who considered that "neutral is the only gender that always suits me," created nongendered self-portraits in a variety of identities that anticipated the invented film stills of Cindy Sherman. The Eluards practiced partner-swapping and indulged frequently in extramarital relations. Nora Mitrani graphically described pleasuring herself before a loved one.[7]

In the event, Breton was not the only one made uncomfortable by sex. In addition to upsetting the Catholic bourgeoisie, as was intended, the Surrealists' attitudes managed to offend the Marxist orthodoxy, for whom sexual matters were a back-burner affair or grounds for squeamishness. Breton sarcastically quoted a French Communist Party official's rebuke, in response to a masturbatory "daydream" by Dalí involving an underage girl and bread dough, that the Surrealists "stank of bourgeois rottenness," and that their "perversions" were "complicating the simple, healthy relations between men and women." "Who dared maintain," an outraged Breton asked, "that, in bourgeois society, these relations were simple, or healthy?"[8] In this, the official was merely following Lenin, who had dismissed "sexual questions" as "a waste of youthful health and strength." "There is no place for it in the Party," he had scolded Clara Zetkin. "Dissoluteness in sexual life is bourgeois, is a phenomenon of decay." And while both Surrealists and Communists reviled the bourgeois family unit and all it stood for, the former's horror of procreation—their avowed preferences ran to such contraceptive positions as sodomy, fellatio, and sixty-nine—put them at odds with the latter, who exhorted women to serve the cause by producing masses of little proletarians.[9]

Despite these differences, Breton maintained that the violence of revolution and the violence of sexual release were two sides of the same coin, or communicating vessels—and in fact, it was in his book *Communicating Vessels* that he advanced: "Only a radical social change whose effect would be to suppress, along with capitalistic production, the very conditions of ownership specific to it could cause reciprocal love to triumph on the level of real life, [since this love stumbles] over economic considerations that are all the more powerful as they are sometimes repressed." In trying to synthesize the power of the libido and the power of social upheaval, Breton was anticipating thinkers such as Reich, or the Herbert Marcuse of *Eros and Civilization:* "In a world of alienation," Marcuse wrote in 1955, "the liberation of Eros would necessarily operate as a destructive, fatal force—as the total negation of the principle which governs the repressive reality." The feminist writer and sociologist Xavière Gauthier credits Surrealism with being the first aesthetic movement to "situate the revolutionary struggle on the side of Eros."[10]

The dangerous power of sexuality has been celebrated and dreaded practically since the dawn of human consciousness, with laws, religious prohibitions, and societal pressures brought to bear as authorities have struggled to maintain their dominance against the anarchic allure of our deepest erotic impulses. Challenges to such institutions as the nuclear family have in particular been met with fury and derision, condemned as attempts to undermine the very bases of civilization. Surrealism, by promoting the subversive power of Eros and making this a repeated focus of its activities and productions, forced into the conversation a number of topics formerly dismissed as taboo or resolutely kept out of bounds, helping pave the way for today's heightened awareness of gender issues and more open sexual politics. But this promotion came with a fair amount of equivocation, which bespeaks both the rage that many Surrealists felt at their upbringing and the strong hold on them that this upbringing nonetheless maintained.

Perhaps nowhere does this equivocation come to the fore as much as when considering the role of women in the Surrealist movement. "The problem of woman is the most wonderful and disturbing problem there is in the world," Breton had written in 1929. Fifteen years later, as the devastation of World War II was nearing an end, he called for a new, matriarchal social order: "May we be ruled by the idea of *the salvation of the earth by woman,* of the transcendent vocation of woman, a vocation which has been systematically concealed, thwarted, or led astray to our day. . . . The time has come to value the ideas of woman at the expense of those of man, whose bankruptcy has become tumultuously evident today."[11]

While statements such as these might seem forward-thinking,

especially for the times, many commentators in the years since have felt that the "problem" was neither wonderful nor had much to do with women, but rather that it lay squarely with the man who had written these lines, and with those who subscribed to them. The English Surrealist painter Ithell Colquhoun, for instance, reflected that despite such pronouncements, "most of Breton's followers were no less chauvinist for all that. Among them, women as human beings tended to be 'permitted not required.'" Leonora Carrington, meanwhile, when I once asked her for her opinion of Surrealism, recalled it simply as "another bullshit role for women."[12]

Consider the evidence: There is René Magritte's well-known canvas from 1929, *I Do Not See the* [*Woman*] *Hidden in the Forest,* depicting a classic painted nude framed by photographic portraits of seventeen Surrealist men: seventeen gazes, made no less male by the fact that the men have their eyes closed (which in itself is telling). Or the many Surrealist visual works depicting the female form dismembered, disfigured, displayed, or otherwise deformed. Or the many written works in which women figure as muse, lover, inspiration, enlightener, sorceress or clairvoyant, torturer or enigma, salvation or apparition, but almost never as an autonomous individual, and all too often as no more than an objectified, sometimes headless, body.* Breton was not the

*One of Max Ernst's collage novels was in fact titled *La Femme 100 têtes,* the homophonic French pun meaning either "the woman with 100 heads" (*cent têtes*) or "the woman without a head" (*sans tête*). The artist Dorothea Tanning, who was married to Ernst, translated the book as *The Hundred Headless Woman.*

only boy in the band who viewed women mainly in terms of his desire: his fondest wish, he once wrote, was to wake up and find "a companion I hadn't chosen" beside him in his hotel bed. Even when that desire was elevated to a philosophical principle, such as in his assertion that marvelous chance encounters "explicitly or not always tend to assume female traits," it often carried an undertone of adolescent fantasy.[13]

So we can understand the frustration and rage that women have expressed toward Surrealism: the more seductive the promise, the more painful the letdown. On the one hand, it claimed to be one of the most woman-focused and erotically free movements in the history of literature and art. Alongside the productions that mutilated women were an equal number that exalted them, or at least the idea of them, as superior beings attuned to natural and supernatural forces beyond the reach of men. Within the movement itself, women often participated in the collective activities and were promised an alternative to the stifling roles that mainstream society expected them to fill.

But all too often, these grand promises fell flat, and in more than one case the women who came to Surrealism as artists and writers with their own talents and ambitions, or who claimed for themselves the same freedoms in lifestyle and beliefs that the men did, were disappointed to encounter obstacles from their own peers that hardly differed from those of society at large. In *Mad Love,* for instance, Breton celebrates (and reproduces) the image of his second wife, Jacqueline Lamba, swimming nude in a fish tank at the Coliséum music hall, a money-gig she held when they met; but he never mentioned her more serious activities as a painter, and threw a fit when on a whim she dyed her hair green, despite its being his favorite color. "I noticed with a certain consternation," Dorothea Tanning related, "that the place of woman in Surrealism was no different than her place in bourgeois society in general." Eileen Agar noted the same double standard when she observed: "Surreal men expected to be very free sexually, but when Lee Miller had the same attitude while with Man Ray, the hypocritical upset was tremendous." And Ithell Colquhoun was expelled from the British Surrealist group because her interest in witchcraft was deemed inappropriate by her male colleagues, who otherwise embraced transgressive antirationalisms.[14]

Still, while it would be easy to brush away Surrealism as just another narcissistic patriarchal exercise that failed to live up to its big claims, perhaps it's more complicated than that. We can start by distinguishing between woman as (male-generated) theory and women as members of the group, though the two are often hard to disentangle. "The problem," writes Gwen Raaberg, "arises out of a situation in which the concepts and principles that focused Breton and other male Surrealists on the female also limited their capacity to view women as independent, active subjects. . . . The concept of 'woman' objectified by male needs was in direct conflict with the individual woman's subjective need for self-definition and free artistic expression."[15]

A perfect illustration of this is the befuddlement many male, and even some female, Surrealists have felt at the cool reception by certain readers to Breton's *Arcanum 17* (1944), which contains the above citation about "*the salvation of the earth by woman.*" How, they wondered, could such a stirring call to liberation and equality be offensive? Similarly, the sentence that immediately follows in the book—"It is artists, in particular, who must take the responsibility . . . to maximize the importance of everything that stands out in the feminine world view in contrast to the masculine, to build only on woman's resources, to exalt, or *even better to appropriate to the point of jealously making it one's own*"[16]—was seen by them as an endorsement, rather than as an erasure of women whose "feminine world view" needs to be reclaimed by the male artist in order to be valued. That said, if readers today can pinpoint, as the Surrealists of the time could not, what is so cringeworthy about such pronouncements, we might also consider that our response is itself an outgrowth of the interrogation of societal attitudes toward gender that the Surrealists, however clumsily, set in motion.

Given the prevailing societal and religious attitudes of the time, which put female sexuality (if it had to be at all) in the service of procreation, Breton's image of woman as spiritually enlightened and sexually adventurous had a distinctly subversive cast. By placing the accent on transgression and pure desire ("the only motive of the world, the only rigor humans must be acquainted with"), he was in fact positing a substantially liberated world, an Eden without the restrictive taint of original sin, "The way the first man loved the first woman / In total freedom."[17]

On the other hand, as Simone de Beauvoir pointed out, sexual liberation is not synonymous with women's emancipation. And Gauthier observes that this supposed rejection of Christian morality is itself deeply Christian, a reaffirmation, beneath the profanation, of the heteronormative couple in all its alleged purity and exclusivity. Breton, though serially involved with several women, saw each of his major love affairs as a realization of predestiny, of the kind of love "that allows itself a whole lifetime, that of course only consents to find its object in one single being."[18] His expression of it in *Mad Love* resorts to terminology straight out of the Gospels: "Only temptation is divine. To feel the need to vary the object of this temptation, to replace it by others—this bears witness that one is about to be found unworthy, that one has already doubtless proved unworthy of *innocence*."[19] Nor was Breton alone in this attitude: Eluard, Dalí, Aragon, Péret, and others besides—in their writings if not always in their actions—promoted the image of a unique love-object, one who, once identified, is "fixed forever," becoming indistinguishable from her male lover. Writes Eluard:

She has the shape of my hands,
She has the color of my eyes,
She dissolves into my shadow . . .[20]

Breton's celebrated poem "Free Union" draws out a long litany of his lover's body that, with its repeated incipit "*Ma femme*" (which can translate as "My woman," "My wife," or, in Mary Ann Caws's rendering, "My beloved"—but the real issue is the possessive pronoun), slowly absorbs the inamorata into the poet's intense gaze:

My woman with her forest-fire hair
With her heat-lightning thoughts . . .
My woman with her sex of placer and platypus
My woman with her sex of seaweed and old-fashioned candies
My woman with her mirror sex
My woman with her eyes full of tears . . .[21]

Times change, and what once sounded romantic and daring threatens to strike modern ears as claustrophobic, in that it leaves the love object little room for personal agency, or as merely corny. It's possible that Breton's breathy panegyrics can no longer hold up against the steely sensibilities of our age, that we're simply more attuned to the scatological Thanatos of sometime-Surrealist Georges Bataille, in perv-porn fictions like *Madame Edwarda, My Mother,* and *Story of the Eye* ("'Put it in my ass, Sir Edmond,' Simone shouted. And Sir Edmond delicately glided the eye between her buttocks. . . . In *Simone's* hairy vagina, I saw the wan blue eye of *Marcelle,* gazing at me through tears of urine.").[22] But we might also see the continuous erotic frenzy of the indissociable union that the Surrealists described as a rebuke to the passionless conventional marriages they witnessed all around them, and in many cases were raised in. Just as we might consider that in the two examples above, though they adopt the subjective viewpoint of the poet ("the color of *my* eyes," "*My* woman"), the implication is of a reciprocal merging: if she dissolves into my shadow, I also dissolve into hers. Perhaps.*

A corollary critique of these romanticizing visions is that they infantilize, and nowhere more blatantly than in the Surrealists' exaltation of the "child-woman" (*femme-enfant*). Part Lolita, part Salome, the child-woman is the distillation of the female principle, a creature of eternal youth and unsettling clairvoyance, an antidote to the rational order that Surrealism had always

*But then, isn't that the pathetic misconception of all romantic love, the stuff of countless sonnets and pop songs? Our hearts beat as one. You are me and I am you. It's one illusion, at least, that the Surrealists didn't invent.

opposed, whose "absolute transparency" could alone counteract "male despotism."[23] Omnipotent though she might be, however, the child-woman remains dependent. Having no role but to inspire the artist with her feminine world view, she is endowed with every ability, allowed every freedom, except that of ignoring (or competing with, still less contradicting) the poet who celebrates her. Péret takes this male ideal of passive devotion even further when he writes that the child-woman "inspires the love of the totally virile man, for she completes him trait for trait. This love reveals her to herself by casting her into a world of marvels, to which she totally abandons herself."[24]

Here again, it's important not to conflate every group member's thinking. René Crevel, in books like *My Body and I* (1925), rebelled against the inherent possessiveness of this mad love, and more generally against the rigid sexual identities that men and women were supposed to inhabit (taking his cue from Sade, whose character Dolmancé proclaims of himself, "It is so sweet to change sex, so delicious to counterfeit the whore, to give oneself to a man who treats us as if we were a woman."). Pierre Molinier painted tangles of black-stockinged, bare-bottomed figures who were cross-dressed versions of himself. Carrington wrote of her own identity, "I was an androgyne, the Moon, the Holy Ghost, a gypsy, an acrobat, Leonora Carrington, and a woman."[25] The power lies in the ambivalence, the multiplicity.

The counterpart to the nurturing child-woman in the movement's female pantheon is the praying mantis, the Delilah, the succubus, the Dalinian "spectre of sex appeal." Gauthier advances the thesis that in Surrealist poetry women are good and adored, while in painting they are evil and abhorred. Though this is hardly systematic, Surrealist visuals do tend to present a vision of the "fair sex" that is harsher, more threatening, or more violent than their verbal counterparts.

But violence can operate on many levels. We create with our desire, and women's bodies have for millennia been depicted in idealized forms that often contain their share of aggression. Is Magritte's *The Rape* (1934), which places a woman's breasts and pubic hair in place of her facial features, indeed rapey? Is Hans Bellmer, with his trussed, disarticulated dolls, or Man Ray, with his distortions and lighting effects (such as in the 1934 photograph *Minotaur*), expressing men's storied ambivalence toward women, or are these artists seeking to convey something artistically and philosophically new? Does the more convincing argument belong to Rudolf E. Kuenzli, who writes, "Faced with the female figure, the male Surrealist fears castration, fears the dissolution of his ego. In order to overcome his fears, he fetishizes the female figure, he deforms, disfigures, manipulates her"?[26] Or to Annie Le Brun, who posits that "Surrealism exalted the most contradictory images of women . . . whose only point in common is to deliver femininity from the prison of its traditional representations"?[27] Either way, it bears remembering that the meaning of the Surrealist message rarely lies on the surface.

More generally, do the contradictions and limitations of the Surrealists' attitudes toward sexuality and gender disqualify them from current debates, or can we use these attitudes to look beyond the normative parameters of their, and our, time? It's a valid question: even in their more benign moments, there is no doubt that most Surrealist collectives were male-dominated and frequently intimidating (though the humbling aspect seems to have affected men as well as women). But while some women in the movement experienced marginalization and dismissal, others felt, at least to some extent, empowered by their affiliation with it. Meret Oppenheim remarked that "for us women, Surrealism represented a world in which we could rebel against the conventions of our upbringing, and in which imagination was a key to a more liberated life"; and she felt that while "the dominance of men in the Surrealist group was the same as everywhere else," for the most part "they accepted women as artists without prejudice." And Penelope Rosemont saw an inherent feminism in the Surrealists' ways of being: "Those involved in Surrealism have championed the feminine, the idea of love, and encouraged women. . . . Surrealists have often called attention to the idea that the progress of civilization could be judged by the way it treats its women and they upheld a belief in Mad Love and sexual experimentation"[28] (though, as discussed above, with caveats). Rosemont also highlights the comparatively large number of women artists and writers who participated in Surrealist activities and discussions, some quite prominently, among them Oppenheim, Leonora Carrington, Dorothea Tanning, Remedios Varo, Joyce Mansour, Lee Miller, Leonor Fini, Jacqueline Lamba, Gisèle Prassinos, Kay Sage, Toyen, Judit Reigl, Annie Le Brun, Nora Mitrani, Mimi Parent, Eileen Agar, Valentine Hugo, Simone Kahn Breton, Alice Rahon, Nelly Kaplan, Valentine Penrose, Ithell Colquhoun, Unica Zürn, and Rosemont herself.

At times the ambiguous and limiting position of women in

Surrealism could itself be a spur to greater agency. Constituting a "minority within a minority,"[29] as Agar put it, they forged their own freedom and tilled their own ground, mapping out an iconography that sometimes sidestepped, sometimes co-opted the images of women produced by men. Paintings such as Carrington's *Self-Portrait* (1937–38) and Tanning's *Birthday* (1942) reinvent representation of the self in ways that differ from male depictions by introducing a more personal symbolism and, in Tanning's case, a direct gaze that talks back to the viewer. Oppenheim's fur-lined cup and saucer, which rivals Dalí's *The Persistence of Memory* as Surrealism's most famous visual and was the first work by a woman to enter the Museum of Modern Art's permanent collection, uses Surrealist tropes to subvert our cozy familiarity with common household items. Leonor Fini, in *Chthonian Divinity Watching Over the Sleep of a Young Man* (1946), reverses the standard order of passive and active, gazer and gazed-upon. The point, in other words, is not to repudiate Surrealism for its failures but rather to identify the moments it offers in which prohibition becomes opportunity, a disruptive force within the movement itself. And if these and other works by women are only recently getting the attention they deserve, how much of this is due to the male-dominated Surrealist clique, and how much to a critical and scholarly establishment that, like the shut-eyed men framing Magritte's picture, would not, could not see the woman artist hanging in the gallery?

It is true that Carrington, Fini, and Sage have not attained the prominence of a Dalí or a Magritte—though exhibitions such as

"Fantastic Women" at the Louisiana Museum in Copenhagen in 2020 and "Surréalisme au féminin?" at the Musée de Montmartre in 2023 might be changing this—and that the poets Mansour and Rahon are not (yet) as canonical as Eluard or Desnos. But I believe it is also true that, as Nancy Joyce Peters notes, the number of women in the movement was "disproportionately large . . . in comparison with token women artists elsewhere." And Peters goes on to say: "Surrealism's allegorical Woman goes much further [than just objectification], as her image becomes multiple, ironic, and mythically complex."[30] The issue is not to settle the debate but rather to delve into its intricacies. Buying wholesale into Surrealist self-promotions as a liberating force for women is just as one-dimensional as knee-jerk rejections of the movement for being baseline misogynistic.

Leonora Carrington recalled that discovering Surrealism as a young woman felt "like a burning inside; you know how when something really touches you, it feels like burning."[31] Lighting that fire, inspiring someone to look beyond their own limitations, is sometimes enough to spark revolutions. Particularly among female artists of the current generation, Surrealism, especially as it was practiced by Carrington, Oppenheim, and others, has provided "an opportunity for painters to more fully realize anxieties and experiences pertaining to womanhood . . . [and] to expand upon visual representations of sex in a way that is more inclusive and attentive to a variety of erotic and emotive expressions." One of these painters, Madeleine Roger-Lacan, commented that "in Surrealism made by women, women's bodies and symbols that have often been used to arouse the viewer are now associated [with] strange and specific personal visions of our womanly experience."[32]

For artists of all genders, Surrealism opened, and continues to open, if only by inches, a door to self-expression, self-invention, and self-identification that refuse traditional categories—including the categories of "men" and "women" artists. Dorothea Tanning, for one, was unequivocal in rejecting these distinctions: "As someone, a human someone, who has chosen art, the making of it, the dedication to it, the breathing of it, this artist has pursued with a high heart that great aim and has utterly failed to understand the pigeonholing (or dove-coterie) of gender, convinced that it has nothing to do with qualifications or goals." Or, as Meret Oppenheim reminded an interviewer, "There is no difference between man and woman; there is only artist or poet."[33]

6 disruption: free radicals

The immediate reality of the Surrealist revolution is not so much to change anything in the physical and apparent order of things as to create a movement in men's minds.

ANTONIN ARTAUD, INTERNAL COMMUNICATION (1925)

Surrealism, in the words of its founder, "began mainly as a protest,"[1] a rebellion against constraints, whether sexual or societal. Though that protest is now known primarily through its artistic and literary incarnations, from practically the moment of the movement's founding, and continuing unabated throughout its history, it also took the form of intense political activism—fueled at first by a revulsion against the world war into which many of the earliest members had been thrown, and spreading into a revolt against oppression and the nationalist and economic mechanisms that fostered it.

It was this feeling of revolt that led the Surrealists, in the mid-1920s, into contact with what would become their main political interlocutors, the Communist International (Comintern) and its French incarnation, the French Communist Party (Parti Communiste Français, or PCF). At first, Surrealism and Communism seemed like natural allies: both were opposed to French imperialism and to war in general; both wanted the overthrow of capitalism, which they saw as corrupt, racist, and soul-deadening; both resisted what Desnos called the "westernization" of the world, embodied by such entities as the newly chartered League of Nations. At a time when the Allied powers were crowing in the wake of the 1918 Armistice, the Surrealists were challenging the very foundations of these attitudes, denouncing their country's colonial wars as imperialist abominations, and taking the destruction of Western culture as their primary mission, by whatever means. Given this, it's not surprising that they should look to Communism as the Great Red Hope, and they were not alone: many other left-leaning French intellectuals of the time, including the prominent novelists Romain Rolland, Henri Barbusse, and André Gide, were weighing degrees of political investment. A survey from 1925, one of several, acknowledged this shift toward politics by asking whether intellectuals could "still confine themselves to an ivory tower, or should they be involved in public affairs?" Yet, as Jonathan P. Eburne, discussing the survey, points out, "Even in this context, Surrealism's political involvement was remarkable for its comprehensiveness."[2]

But fissures soon began appearing in the alliance, and over time the Surrealists—often in opposition to prevailing opinion and influence—would protest restrictive actions regardless of where they lay on the political spectrum, from French involvement in Algeria and French and American incursions in Vietnam to the Soviet invasions of Hungary and Czechoslovakia. When in 1952 Breton characterized Surrealism as "that little particle of free thought,"[3] he was looking back on years of struggle to maintain that freedom of thought against efforts to muzzle or redirect it, not only from conservative thinkers and government institutions but also, and especially, from the same radical Left with which the group had tried persistently to make common cause.

The history of Surrealism's political involvements is rife with conflicting priorities and changes of mind and heart, a tangle of personal rivalries and spites, stumbling attempts to find the right footing, and genuine philosophical differences. In its broadest outlines, it can be summarized as having three phases: an early and enthusiastic embrace of Communist ideals, which the group initially saw as complementary to its own; a more tortuous effort in the 1930s to rebrand Surrealism as a fully fledged Marxist-Leninist entity, in hopes of drawing closer to the Party; and a final break after 1935 with Communism in its Stalinist form, along with attempts to find alternate solutions for meaningful political action. What distinguishes these efforts, at least for some of those involved, is the resolute independence of spirit that guided them. While, to the Communist orthodoxy, the Surrealists' convictions often seemed obtuse and obstructionist (and, to conservative elements, merely ridiculous), and while they led the group down many contradictory paths, a constant tenet was the individual's inalienable right to freedom of mind.

One reason for the Surrealists' uneasy relations with Communism was that their sympathies were ultimately more emotional than practical; unlike most activists, they had no social platform and, with few exceptions, were not interested in holding office. It was the poetry of politics that attracted them, not its machinery. Such a foundation might seem wobbly to those who prefer engagement with cold facts, but isn't political commitment by its very nature visceral and poetic? Though sparked by real-life events, political revolts—whether the Russian Revolution, the May 1968 protests, or Black Lives Matter—get their fire and energy from our rage, hope, aspiration, and despair. The Surrealists were not interested in the reasoned face of protest but in the ardor that sparked it; Breton, who sought the same paroxysms in political action as in love or marvels, later identified "the primacy of passion" as Surrealism's most overriding feature. As an early document put it: "Before any Surrealist or revolutionary preoccupation, what predominates in [our] minds is a certain state of fury. . . . It is by means of this fury that [we] are the most likely to achieve what may be called the Surrealist illumination."[4]

More familiar with literary history than with political science, the Surrealists equated "revolution" with outside-the-box writers like Rimbaud and Lautréamont, or with Saint-Just, Robespierre, and other firebrands of the French Revolution, of which they had a fairly romanticized notion, or with the Paris Commune of 1871. They knew little about Lenin and Trotsky or the Soviet state, and nothing about its back-room maneuverings. Moreover, their first exploratory visit to the PCF offices, shortly after the French Party's founding in 1920, had left them underwhelmed. Aragon later recounted their greeting by a Party official: "The statements this character made, his kind of false bonhomie (he told us: 'There comes a time when you have to go down into the crowd, crush in elbow to elbow, and sweat together'), put us ill at ease. We looked at this overweight creature and had no desire whatsoever to sweat with him." They were also discouraged by the "repellent" bureaucratic requirements for membership. "I cannot believe that many people consider Socialist discipline a necessity," Breton wrote in his diary. "I'd like to know how far its demands go."[5] (He would soon have his answer.)

On top of which, the early Surrealists, fresh off the Dada train, tended toward an anarchistic irreverence that spared neither Left nor Right, making them suspect in the eyes of their putative allies. While their 1924 broadside *A Corpse,* for instance, won the approval of the leftist periodical *Clarté* for its excoriations of the late novelist Anatole France, a Nobel laureate whose "true Gallic temperament" had found favor with both conservatives and progressives, it simultaneously came under fire for a glib rebuff by Aragon against "doddering Moscow," as one of the capitals where France's work was popular. Challenged on this point by *Clarté*'s editor Jean Bernier, Aragon upped the ante by dismissing the Russian Revolution as, "on the scale of ideas, no more than a vague ministerial crisis."[6] Breton, who had been trying to engineer a partnership with *Clarté,* was forced to reprimand his lieutenant in print.

The group's more explicit turn toward political action and the Communist cause came in the summer of 1925, spurred by two main catalysts. The first was a shared disgust at France's role in helping quell an anticolonialist rebellion in the Rif sector of Morocco, an involvement that was as polarizing as the war in Algeria would be in its time. In response, the Surrealists joined with a number of other leftist organizations to help draft the petition "Revolution First and Always!" The tract, a protest against French military intervention, followed an earlier PCF appeal by urging soldiers in the Rif to desert, then went one better by calling for the elimination of Western nations in general: "We find the idea of the fatherland repellent. . . . Wherever Western civilization reigns, all human attachment but that motivated by self-interest has ceased, 'money is the bottom line.'"[7] (This tract also included the above-noted call for "the Mongols [i.e., Soviets] to set up camp in our squares.")

The second catalyst was Breton's reading of Trotsky's 1925 biography of Lenin, which he immediately reviewed for *La Révolution surréaliste* with the passionate terminology of an infatuated convert, praising its "perfect tone" and "brilliant, just, definitive, magnificent pages."[8] He later remarked that "reading such a work sent me into raptures." Within days, his ardor had been communicated to the others, infusing Eluard and even the dandyish Aragon with revolutionary zeal, and for the next several months the group's activities mainly centered on grassroots political action. While they had already recognized "the urgent need for an economic and social upheaval that would put an end to certain glaring inequities," Breton later explained, "until that moment, we had barely given a thought to the *means* of effecting such a transformation."[9] Now, Breton's enthusiasm for Trotsky had brought about a dramatic change in attitude for Surrealism as a whole.

Breton's review is a microcosm of both the power and the failure of Surrealist rhetoric, and of purely inflammatory language in general. On the one hand, his impassioned conviction, coupled with his considerable powers of persuasion, inspired a number of his colleagues toward a level of activism that would help set the course for Surrealism for decades to come, and that in some ways constitutes one of its proudest legacies. On the other, the primacy of fervent assertion over thoughtful reflection forestalled any discussion or objection, eventually resulting in numerous misunderstandings, painful reversals, even suicide.

Indeed, while the attempted rapprochement with Communism was not universally welcomed within the group, neither was dissension tolerated. Soupault, for one, had never been more than lukewarm about this turn of affairs, and in November 1926 he was drummed out of Surrealism for this and a laundry list of other supposed faults. That same month, Artaud was called on the carpet to justify his work in theater and his political views. Asked whether or not he "gave a damn" about the Revolution, he retorted, "I don't give a damn about the kind of revolution you mean"—and was also expelled. Soon after, he attacked his former comrades as "toilet-paper revolutionaries" whose involvement with the Communists had killed Surrealism.[10]

Other Surrealists, meanwhile, were criticizing Breton for not being Communist enough. Several months before the exclusions of Soupault and Artaud, Pierre Naville published a brochure that chided the group for its revolutionary ineffectiveness and "anarchistic attitude." While the movement had recently taken large strides toward "Marxist revolutionary conduct," Naville argued, its vague calls for collaboration between intellectuals and the proletariat still left many practical questions unanswered. "For [the revolution], today, the support of intellectuals can only mean the help of technicians and men accustomed to journalistic tasks. . . . But from poets, thinkers, and artists, the proletariat can expect nothing."[11]

Breton's rebuttal, titled "In Self-Defense," rejected as "wholly artificial" the opposition that both Naville and the Party maintained between inner reality and the factual world:

> There is not one of us who does not hope for the passage of power from the hands of the bourgeoisie to those of the proletariat. In the meantime, we deem it absolutely necessary that inner life should pursue its experiments, and this, of course, without external control, not even Marxist. Doesn't Surrealism, moreover, tend to posit these two states as essentially one and the same?[12]

He also reserved harsh critiques for the PCF house organ *L'Humanité* ("puerile, bombastic, needlessly *cretinizing*") and particularly for its literary editor, best-selling novelist Henri Barbusse, whom he denigrated as a narrow-minded buffoon—further alienating the Party he was ostensibly trying to placate. Perhaps more fundamentally, he pinpointed "certain gaps that all our hopes in Communism's ultimate triumph cannot fill: isn't man implacably the enemy of his fellow man? won't boredom end only when the world does?"[13]

Despite these caveats, Breton and those remaining around him continued to believe that the Surrealist and Communist goals were essentially sympathetic, and that Surrealism had an important role to play in achieving them. But as would become starkly apparent, the two sides were working from vastly different playbooks. The Surrealists were convinced that a true revolution of the human condition must *begin* with a revolution of the mind. For this reason, writers such as Lautréamont, Rimbaud, and Sade, by virtue of their liberated aesthetics and attitudes, had more subversive potential, and more to teach the proletariat, than the retrograde authors prized by the Communist rank and file, like Barbusse, Emile Zola, or the reviled Anatole France. As the historian Helena Lewis remarks, "The Surrealists always maintained that one of the most important ways to undermine capitalism is to destroy the supremacy of bourgeois rationalism."[14] The Surrealists also pointed out, correctly, that many Soviet propaganda books and films upheld the same abhorred bourgeois values of family, country, and labor under a slightly different guise. And they steadfastly maintained their need for autonomy, as a group and as artists, in order to work effectively.

So while the Party "needed intellectuals to run its press, its cultural functions, and to be delegates at international congresses," it accepted the Surrealists' offers of help (when it accepted them at all) as if picking up a filthy handkerchief. As far as the PCF was concerned, the Surrealists' penchant for avant-garde and automatic writing was mere bourgeois intellectual snobbery, and their independent group status deeply suspicious. "If you're a Marxist, you have no need to be a Surrealist," Breton quoted one Party official "bawling" at an applicant. They also found the Surrealists' belief in the reconciliation of dream and waking states—Breton's "certain point of the mind at which life and death, the real and the imagined . . . cease to be perceived as contradictions"—pointless. And they disliked the group's professed admiration for Freud, whose theories about sex offended their puritanical sensibilities. Even the name of the Surrealists' periodical, *La Révolution surréaliste,* was problematic: wasn't there only *one* Revolution? Breton later recounted his occasional summonses to explain himself before Party officials: "Nothing seemed more like a police interrogation. . . . My explanations were deemed satisfactory soon enough, but there was always a moment when one of the inquisitors would brandish a copy of *La Révolution surréaliste* and put everything back in question."[15]

Least convincing of all for the Communists was the argument that intellectual or moral conditions had to be improved before material ones. An article by Paul Nizan criticized the Surrealists for wasting time on "postrevolutionary problems" when the immediate goal was to achieve socialism. But as the Belgian writer Guy Mangeot asked in rebuttal, "How could there be such things as postrevolutionary problems? . . . As if all problems should not be envisaged even before the revolution in order that those who will make it will be completely free!"[16]

Let's pause for a moment on this key philosophical divide. While the Communists often come off in studies of Surrealism as parochial bureaucrats, which many of them indeed were, their objections weren't entirely unfounded. The fact is, the majority of Surrealist works came from a place far outside most laborers' field of reference or interest, and many of these works were (and are) frankly ponderous. Phrases such as "Reason is the plate and the heart the fork. What is the dish?"[17] (from Michel Leiris's 1927 novel *The Cardinal Point*) could easily sound meaningless and insulting to someone struggling to put food on that plate. More broadly, to those who have suffered crushing political and economic oppression, seen family members and comrades in arms murdered by the forces in domination, or grappled against the hardship of maintaining an existence and the sense of futility and despair that can go with it, the Surrealists' insistence on artistic freedom and the revolutionary value of avant-garde writers from a century earlier must have seemed like an infuriating joke, and their proposed solutions to "the principal problems of life" completely out of touch with the daily realities of survival. Not that the Surrealists, for their part, were wrong in warning that a purely economic approach did not address the root causes of human dispossession, as history has borne out many times over. But they were so convinced of their position that they found it impossible to sell the message. In a syndrome familiar to many political parties, including in our own time and place, they were attempting to court a constituency without first learning how to speak its language or address its concerns.

That said, there is a particular clarity in the Surrealists' assertions—such as Breton's "man implacably the enemy of his fellow man"—that rejects easy solutions and slogans, and that credits the uncomfortable truth that, at bottom, the fault might lie not in our political systems so much as in ourselves. One can call it "meritocracy," "dictatorship of the proletariat," "survival of the fittest," or any other quotable phrase. The fact remains that, since the beginnings of recorded humanity and with no plausible end in sight, people have always gravitated toward some kind of hierarchy, generally one that sits themselves and their peers at the top of the pyramid. This is not to disparage or undermine attempts at deconstructing that hierarchy, at questioning its bases and redressing the obscene inequities it has almost always imposed. But to believe that any political system thus far conceived and enacted will wash away those hierarchies smacks of magical thinking. Jenny Holzer's "An elite is inevitable" (*Truism Footstool,* 1988) is both a truism and a warning.

■

poetry
isn't revolution but a way of knowing
why it must come

ADRIENNE RICH, "DREAMWOOD"[18]

With the economic Crash of 1929 and the Depression of the 1930s, the Surrealists' relations with the Communist Party deteriorated even further. If Surrealism was a protest, it was one that believed in its own goals and means of expression—something that the Party, feeling under increased attack at a time when the influence of fascism was growing throughout Western Europe, found hard to stomach. Nor did its leaders care for the increasingly frequent and pointed criticisms of the PCF's leadership and policies.

Committed still and all to the ideal of social revolution, the Surrealists kept trying to adhere more closely to the Party line, or at least to their idealized vision of it, and to convince the Communists of their orthodoxy. They had already gone out of their way to claim (somewhat disingenuously) that "there was never a Surrealist theory of Revolution," as a declaration they published in *L'Humanité* put it, adding that "when it comes to realizing the Revolution, there can be no question of a 'Surrealist group' as such."[19] In 1927, Breton and four others had petitioned for membership in the Party, and were briefly admitted—although Breton was immediately put off by his first assignment, a report on the coal-mining industry in Fascist Italy. And in 1930, they rebranded *La Révolution surréaliste* as *Le Surréalisme au service de la Révolution* (Surrealism in the Service of the Revolution), featuring on page 1 of the first issue their pledge of allegiance to the Third International.

But despite these concessions, the group's independent streak remained evident, and for every gain there seemed to be another setback, their protestations of good faith constantly undercut by actions that provoked the Communists' suspicion. As Helena Lewis puts it, they "simply assumed that all that was needed to dispel the Party's hostility toward them were repeated assurances of their good will."[20] What they failed to see was how statements such as Breton's rejection of "external control . . . even Marxist," spoke much more loudly to a Party ever with an ear out for strains of dissent. In love with the idea of revolution and the elimination of bourgeois morals, but unable to abide the bureaucratic nature of orthodox Communism, the Surrealists persisted in their dogged attempts at solidarity, but only managed to further convince the Party that they were merely dissident troublemakers.

Several other key factors played into Breton's final break with the Party and with Soviet Communism in general. The first was what became known as the Aragon affair. For more than a decade, Aragon had been Breton's closest confidant and lieutenant and one of Surrealism's most verbally gifted ambassadors—and so, when he was invited, through his relationship with the well-connected Russian novelist Elsa Triolet, to represent the Surrealists at the Congress of Revolutionary Writers in Kharkov, Ukraine, in late 1930, it seemed an invaluable opportunity. Aragon's first dispatches back home, with their enthusiastic accounts of the favor shown Surrealist ideas, seemed to bear this out, and were welcomed in Paris with equal excitement. But as he was leaving the USSR after the Congress, Aragon was notified that in order for the Surrealists to have any role in the Comintern, he would have to sign a document renouncing most of the movement's positions, including those expressed in Breton's recently published *Second Manifesto,* as well as their admiration for Freud. Aragon signed, then went home and repudiated his repudiation to Breton and his French colleagues. He spent the following year vacillating between Surrealism, Triolet's political ambitions for him, and the prestige he'd been made to feel as a flattered delegate in Kharkov.

Matters came to a head when Aragon published an inflammatory propaganda poem, "Red Front" ("Bring down the cops Comrades . . . / I sing the violent domination of the bourgeoisie by the Proletariat"), and was indicted for incitement to murder, which carried a possible prison term of five years. Although the work's artistic merits were debatable at best, Breton wrote a pamphlet in support of Aragon, *The Poverty of Poetry: The "Aragon Affair" and Public Opinion* (1932), in which he tried to defend the work on the shaky grounds that it was merely a poem and not a literal call to action. Aragon, who had already begun chafing under Breton's leadership, and who didn't appreciate seeing his rousing propaganda piece dismissed as mere literature, abandoned Surrealism and joined the PCF heart and soul, driving a major wedge between the two camps. "I had to break with these men who always had the word 'revolution' on their lips, yet for whom there were things more precious than the Revolution itself," he claimed, though the nostalgic cast of his later recollections of Breton and Surrealism tell a different story.[21]

In 1934, the two camps hit a further road bump when the Soviet critic Andrei Zhdanov introduced the doctrine of Socialist Realism, which asserted that the only function of art was to serve the proletarian revolution—humor, dreams, and automatist folderol need not apply. This was in direct contradiction to the position maintained by Breton, who the following year argued to a Communist caucus that "one of our first duties on the literary plane is to shelter such works *full of sap* [that is, the avant-garde writings the Surrealists had always cherished] against all falsification from the right or from the left." For him, the true revolutionary value of a work had to do with its originality and innovative language, not with being a rehash of bromides about the sanctity of labor and five-year plans. As early as 1925, he had advanced that "a work is revolutionary not if it borrows revolutionary ideas from the moral or social sphere, but if it destroys accepted forms or ways of thinking in the domain of aesthetics or logic." The new discipline of Socialist Realism, as he would later characterize it, was merely a form of "mental extermination."[22]

Yet another wedge was driven by the Communist-sponsored Congress of Writers for the Defense of Culture in 1935. Breton had originally been among the scheduled speakers, who also included a large international roster of prominent antifascist intellectuals, but this ran aground after his encounter with the Soviet writer and organizing committee member Ilya Ehrenburg. The year before, Ehrenburg had published a study of contemporary

French literature in which he castigated the Surrealists for being "too busy studying pederasty and dreams [and] spending their inheritances or their wives' dowries"[23] to wage revolution. When Breton happened upon Ehrenburg on the eve of the Congress, he slapped him repeatedly across the face—and was summarily stripped of his invitation to speak. René Crevel, one of the few to maintain good relations with both the Surrealists and the PCF, lobbied strenuously on Breton's behalf, but the Surrealists were finally reinstated only after Crevel, despairing of making any headway, hanged and gassed himself—and even then, Breton's speech had to be delivered not by him but by Eluard, and not until after midnight, by which time most of the delegates had gone home.

As it happened, the committee had reason to block Breton, for his speech directly challenged the twin banners under which the Congress had been staged: the doctrine of Socialist Realism and the recently signed Franco-Soviet Treaty of Mutual Assistance. The pact, which even many loyal Communists found shocking, codified Stalin's endorsement of French rearmament against Germany—something that Breton, who maintained that the alliance of revolutionary Russia with "ultra-imperialist France" could only lead to fatal compromise, had opposed from the outset.* Finally, he reaffirmed Surrealism's unaltering belief in the revolutionary necessity of artistic freedom: "It is not by stereotyped declarations against fascism and war that we will manage

*Breton's attitude might seem frivolous, given the real fascist threat, but his skepticism was borne out in 1939 when Stalin signed the Nazi-Soviet Nonaggression Pact, temporarily allying himself with Hitler.

to liberate either the mind or man from the ancient chains that bind him or the new chains that threaten him." And he ended with what has become one of his most celebrated pronouncements: "'Transform the world,' Marx said; 'change life,' Rimbaud said. These two watchwords are but one for us."[24]

Stirring as his rhetoric might have been, it was evident that any chance for meaningful collaboration with organized Communism was gone. In a postmortem on the Congress published soon afterward, Breton made clear that while the Surrealists continued to think of themselves as revolutionaries, they did not intend "to be forced to give up anything that appears valuable to us and proper to us" simply on the say-so of Stalin, who had turned Soviet Russia "into the very negation of what it should be." Speaking to an interviewer decades later, he pinpointed the Congress as the episode that "finally toppled the hopes that for years, despite everything, we'd had for reconciling Surrealist ideas with practical revolutionary action."[25]

> All the water in the ocean is not enough
> to wash away an intellectual bloodstain.
> ISIDORE DUCASSE, *Poésies* (1870)

Breton's final rift with Soviet Communism came in 1936 with the so-called Moscow Trials. In the fall of that year, Stalin's prosecutor Andrei Vyshinsky staged the first of several now infamous show trials, in which he sentenced a large number of original Bolsheviks, his boss's former comrades in arms, to a cursory bullet in the back of the head. In September, Breton addressed a large rally to denounce the trials as "an abject police undertaking," and Stalin himself as "the great negator and principal enemy of the proletarian revolution . . . the most inexcusable of murderers."[26] He was one of comparatively few leftist intellectuals in France at the time to openly criticize the proceedings, even as the PCF did its best to justify the goings-on in Moscow. Increasingly at odds with the mainstream Left, estranged from former comrades who had embraced fascism, Breton and those still with him had few remaining allies in France. (Somewhat paradoxically, the movement's international presence grew significantly beginning in this period—but then, no one is a prophet in his own land.) The following year, Breton decried the Stalinists' orchestrated campaign of terror and murder against Trotskyist forces in the Spanish Civil War, even though both sides were ostensibly fighting alongside each other to combat Franco's fascists. From this point on, he would become only more disgusted with the revolutionary land he had once so admired.

In 1938, Breton further sealed his defiance of Stalin by traveling to Mexico to visit the exiled Leon Trotsky, who by that point had been targeted by Moscow for assassination (and who would be murdered by a Stalinist agent two years later). Hosted by Diego Rivera and Frida Kahlo, Breton and his wife, Jacqueline Lamba, spent four months living in Rivera's house in the fashionable Mexico City suburb of San Ángel, from where he visited Trotsky as often as the Russian's schedule allowed. Trotsky's stated positions on artistic freedom, in sharp contrast to what Breton had been hearing from PCF officials, seemed to align perfectly with the Surrealists' own. "One cannot without revulsion and horror read the poems and novels or view the paintings and sculptures in which bureaucrats armed with pen, brush, or chisel, supervised by bureaucrats armed with revolvers, glorify the 'great leaders of genius,'" he wrote around the time of Breton's visit. "Art can be the Revolution's greatest ally only insofar as it remains true to itself."[27]

The two men spent hours debating the nature of politics and aesthetics, which resulted in the co-written manifesto "For an Independent Revolutionary Art." The manifesto's major thrust was the affirmation of artistic autonomy that Breton had been unable to obtain from the Stalinists: "To those who would urge us, whether for today or for tomorrow, to consent that art should submit to a discipline which we hold to be radically incompatible with its nature, we give a flat refusal." In an excess of zeal, Breton had also thought to include Trotsky's own proscription: "Complete freedom for art, *except against the proletarian revolution.*" But Trotsky, who too often had seen this latter caveat misused by his former comrades, deleted the exception. The manifesto concluded with Breton's dual injunction: "Our aims: The independence of art—for the revolution; The revolution—for the complete liberation of art!"[28]

Breton left Mexico with further plans for collaborative action, including an international Trotskyist federation, but between the dominance of the Stalinist party in France, the outbreak of World War II, and Trotsky's assassination in 1940, none of these came to fruition. Instead, he broke with still more of his colleagues over politics, most notably with Eluard, who during Breton's time in Mexico had unexpectedly rejoined his old frenemy Aragon on the Stalinist side. "Suddenly, just like that, a friendship ended that had been growing for years, to the point of making us like brothers," Breton lamented.[29]

Following the French defeat in June 1940, a number of Surrealists were forced into hiding. Aragon, Eluard, and René Char worked underground for the Resistance. Others, including Breton, Lamba, Tanguy, Ernst, Tanning, Carrington, Masson, Sage, Péret, Matta, Varo, Rahon, and Paalen, managed to get out of France and spent the war years in exile, many of them in the United States or Mexico. For them, it was a fallow time politically, largely due to the precariousness of their status as refugees and the conditions of their asylum. Breton maintained Surrealist activity as best he could, holding gatherings of geographically scattered members as logistics allowed (one wonders what he might have done with Zoom or FaceTime), and publishing a new Surrealist periodical with Marcel Duchamp called *VVV.* He also lent his services to the Voice of America propaganda broadcasts as an on-air announcer. And he delivered occasional lectures, including the one to the students at Yale University in 1942 in which he reaffirmed his lifelong commitment to freedom and to the young:

> Right now the future rests in the hands of youth, and of youth alone. Surrealism, I say it again, sprang from an affirmation of boundless faith in the *genius* of youth. . . . Freedom: however crudely one may have tried to misuse this word, it is still completely uncorrupted. . . . From one war to the next, one may say that the passionate quest for freedom has been the constant motive of Surrealist action.[30]

But despite such assurances, it was hard for most to credit Surrealism as a vibrant force for change. Particularly in the United States, where Surrealism had always been viewed as primarily artistic, the impact of its visuals was being eroded by Surrealist-inspired American artists like Peter Blume, Helen Lundeberg, and John Wilde, who could convey the movement's styles but not its urgency, or by the self-parodying antics of the ubiquitous Dalí, about whom a *New York Times* critic wrote in 1945 that he had made Surrealism "as comfortable as a pair of scuffed old-fashioned slippers. . . . He has put Surrealism in curl papers for the night and given it a glass of milk."[31]

The situation was not much better in France. When Breton returned in 1946, he found that the French Communist Party, as Stalinist as ever, had only gained in prestige owing to its association with the Resistance, with Aragon and Eluard now enjoying prominent positions; while the Surrealists—still proclaiming their defiance of the PCF, criticized for having left France during the Occupation, and largely ignored by a younger generation more attracted to cooler new trends like jazz and Existentialism—had become further marginalized. I can only imagine Breton's dismay, upon his long-awaited homecoming, at realizing that the movement he'd worked so hard to keep on the abrasive cutting edge was now considered passé.

Which is not to say that the Surrealists were politically inactive after the war. The decades of the late 1940s through the 1960s brought involvements with such entities as the anarchists and the antinationalist World Citizenship Movement (later the World

Service Authority) and Front Humain, as well as statements and interventions on numerous topical events. Notably, the group was largely instrumental in the "Declaration of the 121" against the Algerian War, which directly echoed the 1925 manifesto supporting the Rif rebellion. But in the main, the Surrealists' actions seem less consequential than they once had, perhaps because of their decreased visibility, or because they, like much of the world, had emerged from World War II shocked into numbness. As René Magritte observed to Breton, "The confusion and panic that we wanted to create in order to put everything continually into question . . . were achieved much better by the recent war than by us."[32] Herbert S. Gershman pinpoints this sense of futility among the postwar group: "Having no large following and refusing to proselytize, at best [the Surrealists] could function as gadflies—and gadflies are rarely welcome. Invariably in the minority and having no effective power, they were never responsible for decisions taken elsewhere by others."[33]

In the wake of the Holocaust and the atomic bomb, Breton turned his attention to finding a way out of the "foul corridor through which contemporary man is making his way [which] represents the passage between the so-called universe of concentration camps . . . and a quite possible nonuniverse."[34] Disillusioned with Communism, opposed to both the capitalist and fascist alternatives, and with Trotsky dead, he tried to forge his own morally defensible political path. This time, he sought guidance less from political activists than from esoteric thinkers like the eighteenth-century poet-philosopher Claude Helvétius, whose work influenced Marx's concept of historical materialism, and the nineteenth-century utopian socialist Charles Fourier. His aim was to look past the temporary gains of whichever dictatorship, fascist or proletarian, happened to be in power at the moment; for as he saw it, those gains inevitably led to compromise and bloodshed. Instead, he tried to avoid the either/or trap of capitalism vs. socialism, Right vs. Left, emphasizing human interests over political ones, keeping free of partisan demands so that he wouldn't find himself having to justify either military invasions of Eastern Bloc countries or economic invasions by Disney and Coca-Cola.

Many have written off the Surrealists' attempts at political action as a long-running failure, at best the well-intentioned fumblings of petty-bourgeois dilettantes, at worst a pernicious undermining of serious revolutionary efforts. But there is a lesson to be drawn from their integrity (a word one doesn't often get to associate with politics), and from their unwavering devotion to an honorable set of ideals. The fact that at least some of them upheld the movement's original belief in the coexistence of revolution and liberty, resisting repressiveness on both sides of the political divide, bespeaks a higher lucidity and courage. While their consistency sometimes played them false, it also prevented them from making the same kinds of compromises as many other intellectual figures of the time—whether turning hard Right, like Emmanuel Berl and Pierre Drieu la Rochelle, or, like the PCF, doing handsprings to justify such constantly changing winds from the East as the Franco-Soviet Treaty of Mutual Assistance of 1935, the Nazi-Soviet Nonaggression Pact of 1939, the execution of Czech intellectuals in 1950, the Soviet invasions of Czechoslovakia in 1948 and of Hungary in 1956, and Khrushchev's infamous revelations about Stalin at the Twentieth Party Congress.

Today, as we continue to debate the abolition of capitalism, largely agreeing on its ills but less so on how to remedy them, which is one secret of its longevity, it's worth revisiting the Surrealists' particular brand of activism. At considerable personal, financial, political, and reputational cost, they often saw the ugly underside of political action, and were not afraid to speak it. Gershman, though among those dubious about the Surrealists' ultimate achievements, nonetheless recognizes an essential success in Breton's political engagements: "Despite the many scorners, his was a voice for decency, a visionary, impossible decency perhaps, but decency nonetheless"[35]—no small claim in an arena where the most reprehensible behaviors, then as now, often reap the greatest rewards.

7 revolution: why surrealism matters

Much of the power of Surrealist rhetoric does not survive translation. . . . But the freeing of imagination by the Surrealists remains a tremendous achievement. Beyond the froth—the ideological absurdities, the rampant narcissism, the window display and chic décor—Surrealism remains one of the century's noblest proposals of liberty.

ROBERT HUGHES,
TIME MAGAZINE (1978)

On May 2, 1968, disputes between students and officials at the University of Paris, in the northwest suburb Nanterre, led the administration to shut down the campus, an action that was met with energetic protests. The following week, a march in Paris involving twenty thousand students and their supporters escalated into violent confrontations between demonstrators and police that led to hundreds of arrests, and by midmonth, more than a million people were marching through the streets of the city. The period of unrest and general strikes that began in early May eventually lasted nearly two months, involving some eleven million students, teachers, workers, trade unionists, and sympathizers of all kinds, and virtually paralyzing the nation. Its historical, institutional, cultural, and emotional repercussions echo to this day.

Among the graffitied slogans that sprouted on the façades of office buildings and seats of higher learning during the events of May '68, many of which have since become legendary—"All power to the imagination," "Beneath the paving stones, the beach"—a number turned out to be Surrealist or pro-Surrealist statements: "Choose life instead," "Long live the Surrealist Revolution," "Beauty will be convulsive or will not be" (the concluding sentence of Breton's *Nadja*), while the "Letter to the Rectors of European Universities" from 1925 was posted on the walls of the Sorbonne. And, just as Rimbaud was said to have mounted the barricades of the Paris Commune almost a century earlier, so a number of Surrealists went down into the streets—the streets that Breton had once designated as his "true element [where he] could test like nowhere else the winds of possibility"—to lend a hand. A hastily issued tract put the Surrealist movement "at the students' disposal for any practical action aimed at creating a revolutionary situation."[1]

But as the group was soon forced to recognize, May '68, in many ways the greatest public explosion of Surrealism since its inception, also signaled the movement's decline as an organized entity. "The events of May 1968," said late-generation Surrealist Claude Courtot, "which one could see as Surrealism in the streets, by the same token meant that it no longer remained within the confines of the group. We were almost ejected from it. We felt we had been 'passed on the left,' so to speak."

Moreover, once the general euphoria had died down, the Surrealists were forced to contend with tensions that had been rising since Breton's death a year and a half earlier, in September 1966. It soon became clear that only he had had the personal prestige and intellectual breadth to hold together the various, at times antagonistic, factions within the movement. "Once there was no more Breton," said Courtot, "it all came apart. No one had the necessary authority to chart a course for the ship."[2]

In February 1969, after several more months of schisms and internal dissent, Jean Schuster, Breton's literary executor and designated successor, officially disbanded the French Surrealist group.

In an article published in the French newspaper of record *Le Monde,* Schuster admitted that "the absence of any internal cohesion" made it impossible to pursue the Surrealist adventure as it had been for the past decades. "For all that, is Surrealism dead? No . . . [Surrealism] designates both an ontological component of the human mind . . . and the historically determined movement, which has recognized [this component] and taken it upon itself to exalt, enrich, and arm it in preparation for triumph."[3] While "historical" Surrealism might be coming to an end, Schuster asserted, "eternal" Surrealism, the impulses and energies that had driven it since the beginning, lived on. Moreover, Schuster was really speaking only of the canonical Paris group when he posited the end of "historical" Surrealism: other groups, in Latin America, North America, Scandinavia, and even France, remained active.

What Schuster and Courtot were experiencing was a phenomenon to which, sooner or later, all disruptive movements fall prey: the moment when its programs and precepts take on independent life and no longer need their progenitors to push them forward. The more successful the disruption, the more it becomes assimilated, accepted, and provokes its own end—something Breton had already foreseen in 1942 from his wartime exile in New York, when he wrote: "Any idea that prevails is hastening its own downfall."[4] And in that tumultuous month of May 1968, John Ashbery expressed a similar judgment in his review of the legendary, and legendarily decried, exhibition "Dada, Surrealism, and Their Heritage" at New York's Museum of Modern Art: "Revolutions happen only once. The Surrealist Revolution cannot happen again because it is no longer necessary. We all 'grew up Surrealist' without even being aware of it. . . . Surrealism, as its originators hoped it would, immediately spread to all levels of life."[5]

Not everyone took so benign a view of Surrealism's purported demise. Guy Debord, a founding member of the Situationist International, one of several movements that had sprung up after the war in direct descendance from Surrealism, was already burying the father in the late 1950s as "thoroughly boring and reactionary. Surrealist dreams are mere bourgeois impotence, artistic nostalgia, and a refusal to envisage the liberating use of our era's technological means."[6] But what Debord and others like him failed to recognize was that, while Surrealism in its late manifestations did rail against such modern technological developments as atomic energy and the space race (and what would the Surrealists have made of artificial intelligence?), what it really condemned were the deadening effects of consumer society, which technology served and facilitated. "The revolution which will end the capitalist regime and the society which will take over from it will be neither proletarian nor socialist [but] technocratic," the Surrealist Philippe Audoin predicted in 1965, nearly twenty years before this "silent revolution" became fully evident:

> "Consumer societies" can be predicted gradually to abandon traditional forms of coercion so as to place their faith exclusively on the intimate complicity of their slaves. . . . The artificial creation of needs (which in the course of production have to be satisfied before they have even been felt) by means of advertising drivel, the delirious promotion of the everyday object, the hypnotic effect

of "audio-visual" media, is no doubt the most striking example of this. . . . All of this contributes to diverting Desire from its own ends towards substitutive satisfactions which claim to bring happiness.[7]

In their rejection of the trappings of modern life, especially the religion of technology whose adherents cross over nations and classes, the Surrealists were not promoting "nostalgia," as Debord charged, but rather sounding a prescient warning that the "technological means" he championed as "liberating" could also be used to dominate and control—a warning that today needs no further comment.

To return to our initial questions, then: Why should Surrealism matter today, and what lessons can be drawn from it? Has the movement ended, or does it continue? In either case, why does it still exert such a hold on our imaginations? How has it (and has it) paved the way for a greater acceptance of so-called marginal currents in art, literature, and society?

As a "historical" movement, to use Schuster's term, and despite pockets of activity still ongoing in parts of the world, it would be hard to maintain that Surrealism continues to manifest itself as it had in the interwar years, or even in the decades following World War II. But that's not the point. By resolutely refusing conformity and absorption, in its spirit if not always in its expressions, Surrealism acts as a prototype for historic and aesthetic upheavals in its wake, including those of the current moment. As one recent article put it, "Surrealism bequeaths to us a playful—yet penetrating—set of tools that may as well have been invented for today's world."[8] And while Surrealism can claim few successes in terms of concrete public policy, the "higher lucidity" I have spoken of stands as a model for rebellions wishing to avoid the frequent trap of partisanship and sectarianism, with all the fatal compromises they inevitably entail.

In the realm of aesthetics, the Surrealists constantly sought out new forms in their attempts to preserve and transmit the emotional charge of disruption, which kept the movement from becoming a mere school or style—though, again, the very power of those forms also made them prone to imitation, repetition, and eventually to sterility. But then, the constant need to seek out new means of expression—and, more important, to break down the walls that had long cloistered those means (something that we now take for granted)—is itself an innovative and self-regenerating source of creative energy. Moreover, in highlighting artistic forms that were collective and anonymous, the Surrealists, as Helena Lewis notes, "succeeded in creating an anti-elitist art that acquired a new social meaning."[9]

More generally, Surrealism's embrace and intermingling of a wide range of concerns formerly considered disparate reframes our notion of what those expressive means could do. Breton might have been overreaching when he told an interviewer, "If we refer back to the title of a magazine like *La Révolution surréaliste,* which at the time seemed hyperbolic, it's no exaggeration to say that such a revolution did take place in men's minds."[10] But as Michel Foucault points out, he helped redefine how such a revolution might be effected. Breton's contribution, says Foucault, was to discover "a space that is not that of philosophy, nor of literature, nor of art, but that of experience. We are now in a time when experience—and the thought that is inseparable from it—are developing with an extraordinary richness, in both a unity and a dispersion that wipe out boundaries of provinces that were once well established."[11]

While on some levels that experience might seem scarcely changed from the Surrealists' heyday—the racial and economic disparities they decried still exist, wars still rage, gender inequality remains, fundamentalist religions and their abuses still hold sway over large populations in both East and West—our ability to view these ills with a more jaundiced eye, to radically interrogate the irrationalities of our so-called "rational" world and (however gradually) to remedy them, owes much to Surrealism's heady and creative synthesis of Marxist analysis, Freudian excavation, and Rimbaldian irreverence. Though it was unable to "transform the world" and "change life"—indeed, says the novelist Julien Gracq, though the world has worsened still further as market interests increasingly dominate human activity—it has nonetheless managed "to infuse [life] with fresh air."[12]

The early Surrealists sought to weaponize irrationality against the logical structures that had brought about the first mass technological war, and their brand of irrationality, or some version of it, is a tool that we today might mobilize against a society that fosters increasing inequities and could soon destroy the planet. Exactly how we do it is a question that I throw back at whoever is reading this. Revolts are cyclical, and their methods must remain fluid. The cultural commentator Rex Weiner forecast this in 1977, when he gauged that "Surrealism has no place in the 1970s, for its lessons have been learned too well. . . . The truth is, surrealism is irrelevant today. But in ten years it will happen all over again."[13]

That said, there is a generational paradox at work. Surrealism was a high point of modernism, but we now live, or so we're told, in a postmodern world. Breton begins *Nadja* with the fundamental question, "Who am I?" We might say that the entire modernist enterprise revolves around this question, as well as its pendants, "What is reality?" and "How should I live?" Today, the question is more likely to be, "What does it matter?" (a question encoded in the very title of this book, and of the series in which it's being published). Can the issues the Surrealists grappled with help us navigate our way not only through solving the challenges of the twenty-first century but also through the obstacles we now face—as they did not—in believing that solutions are even possible, which is perhaps the biggest challenge of all?

And there's a personal aspect to it as well. As someone who effectively began his writing career with a book about Breton, and who has been wrestling with and questioning the words and achievements of Surrealism for more than forty years, I can't help feeling implicated in discussions of its relevance. But beyond this: As someone who lives amid a population that is increasingly younger than I am, and whose priorities and attitudes define themselves according to criteria sometimes very different from the ones of my generation—even though, I'm convinced of it, we felt the same fervor for change and social betterment, the same disillusion at the slowness with which they occurred (when they occurred)—I can't help wondering to what extent *I* matter to the current world. And ultimately, what does relevance even mean? Who puts the expiration stamp on this most perishable of cultural products?

Fashions, priorities, urgencies change over time. Many figures who were once considered vital references barely register a blip today, while others who were ignored in their lifetimes have come up for reevaluation. The brightish youngish writer I was in my twenties and thirties is not the person I currently am. I like to think I've developed with age and experience, but I also have to face the reality that I and my peers are not as eternally relevant as we thought we were. Like every generation, we were all about sweeping aside those who were the age I am now, and now that I *am* that age, I increasingly feel the undertow pulling me out to sea to make room for the next wave. The young men and women who originated the Surrealist group in the 1920s were of a similar mind vis-à-vis their predecessors, and the students who went down into the streets in the spring of 1968 no doubt felt that way about the middle-aged Surrealists elbowing in to join them. The world turns, and as Breton was already saying in 1940, "It's useless to try to outlast one's time."[14]

Any artistic or intellectual movement born of a vital impulse, whether Dada, Surrealism, the Situationist International, Fluxus, or what have you, draws its energy from a specific, unique conjunction of personalities, interests, talents, accidents, contexts, and historical events. Any attempt to revisit and explicate that impulse after the fact can do no better than to rediscover for itself the molten core, or else risk draining the subject of its substance and its interest. Robert Storr once penned a salubriously subversive caveat that should be heeded by anyone seeking to understand what Surrealism is about:

> We cannot go back. Academics cannot recapture or reconstitute the mysteries of Surrealist practice by art historical means. Nor can ardent evocations of the original mystique and the credulity upon which they depend revive its spirit. Not everything about Surrealism has aged well. Aspects of its method and rhetoric strike the contemporary reader or viewer as embarrassingly out-of-date, if not preposterous. Acknowledging this fact rather than evading or explaining it away is the necessary first step toward relocating and reconnecting with Surrealism's critical and imaginative essence.[15]

There is no formula for this. It is much harder to recognize how it does happen than how it does not: for example, by assimilating the movement and its participants into a smoothly contoured chronological flow, or by quarantining Surrealism's totalizing embrace into well-established categories, or subsuming it in scholarly anatomization and art historical displays. Or else by letting it be co-opted and denatured by pop cultural approximations, such as the ones I mentioned at the outset, so that it comes to mean everything and nothing. The more this occurs, the more its vitality fades from view, and our ability to reconnect with its critical and imaginative essence grows all the more tenuous. A number of Surrealist writers opened a door to forms of criticism, now coming into their own, that stem not from the head but from the heart and guts. It is a lesson from which the full benefits are yet to be derived.

Surrealism was launched in the wake of unprecedented mass

devastation, but its founders could not fully envision, other than in literary terms, the global annihilation that nuclear warfare and climate change have now made entirely plausible, some would even say likely. If we in the twenty-first century are to access Surrealism meaningfully, it will not be by re-creating the old debates or melting still more watches. Rather, it will be by taking the energy and passion of the movement and adapting it to our present reality, our present surreality. The Surrealists envisioned a world in which existence was infused with marvels and desire, the life-choosing thrill of libido, the mind-popping wonder of fresh discovery, and in which the pleasure principle became the guiding motivator of our daily actions and a path to human salvation, here and now. In the final account, the success or failure—the success *and* failure—of the Surrealist revolution has little to do with how the poetry sounded or the paintings looked. It has to do with commitment to a shared set of ideals, and with how those ideals—whether glimpsed through words, pigment, celluloid, or political action—could reshape our mental processes and ways of living. The aspiration remains, as do the clues that Surrealism has left for us along that path, if we choose to follow it.

notes

INTRODUCTION

1. "Open Letter to André Breton on the Relation of Surrealism to the Grand Jeu," in René Daumal, *The Powers of the Word: Selected Essays and Notes, 1927–1943,* ed. and trans. Mark Polizzotti (San Francisco: City Lights Books, 1991), 56 (trans. revised).

2. Breton's address at Yale was published as "The Situation of Surrealism Between the Two Wars," in Breton, *Free Rein,* 54.

3. *Manifesto of Surrealism* (1924), in Breton, *Manifestoes of Surrealism* (hereafter *Manifestoes*), 26.

4. Alfred H. Barr Jr., *Fantastic Art, Dada, Surrealism,* exh. cat. (New York: Museum of Modern Art, 1936), 8.

5. Quoted in D'Alessandro and Gale, *Surrealism Beyond Borders,* 14. See also the Portuguese Surrealist Mário Cesariny's remark, "One can be a Surrealist without having read Breton. You can read Breton and not be surreal" (ibid., 18).

6. "A Tribute to Antonin Artaud," in Breton, *Free Rein,* 78 (trans. revised).

7. The past few years alone have seen "Fantastic Women" at the Louisiana Museum in Copenhagen (2020), "British Surrealism" at the Dulwich Picture Gallery in London (2020), "Surrealism Beyond Borders" at the Metropolitan Museum of Art in New York and Tate Modern in London (2021–22), "The Milk of Dreams" at the Venice Biennale

(2022), and "Objects of Desire" at the Design Museum, London (2022), among many others, as well as monographic shows devoted to a number of Surrealist artists, some of them household names, others only now being properly assessed.

ONE: WHAT IS SURREALISM?

1. Breton, *Conversations,* 238.

2. All quotations in this paragraph are from the *Manifesto,* 3–4, 14, 18, 26, 32, and 47. The assertions about "living and ceasing to live" and "real life" are direct borrowings from Alfred Jarry and Arthur Rimbaud.

3. Preface to *Les Mamelles de Tirésias,* in Guillaume Apollinaire, *Œuvres poétiques,* ed. Marcel Adéma and Michel Décaudin (Paris: Gallimard / Bibliothèque de la Pléiade, 1965), 865–66. In the *Manifesto* (24), Breton acknowledges that he adopted the term "in homage to Guillaume Apollinaire."

4. "What Is Surrealism?" (lecture from June 1934), in Breton, *What Is Surrealism?,* 118.

5. Georges Charbonnier, *Entretiens avec André Masson,* quoted in Spector, *Surrealist Art and Writing,* 10.

6. Author interviews with Mary Jayne Gold, May 16, 1989, and Monique Fong, January 12, 1988.

7. Quoted in Alain Virmaux and Odette Virmaux, *André Breton qui êtes-vous?* (Paris: La Manufacture, 1987), 72.

8. Sarane Alexandrian, *Breton par lui-même* (Paris: Editions du Seuil, 1971), 170.

9. See André Thirion, *Revolutionaries Without Revolution,* trans. Joachim Neugroschel (New York: Macmillan, 1975), 176–77: "Breton visited the café as if it were an office, with businesslike efficiency." For biographies of Breton in English, see Polizzotti, *Revolution of the Mind,*

and Balakian, *André Breton*. For overviews of his life and work, see Caws, *André Breton,* and the introduction to Polizzotti, ed., *André Breton: Selections.* The two main histories of Surrealism available in English are Maurice Nadeau's chatty but enlightening *History of Surrealism,* which stops at 1945, and Gérard Durozoi's more substantial but relentlessly pedantic *History of the Surrealist Movement.*

10. Breton, *Conversations,* 84.

11. Breton's letters to Simone Kahn were later preserved by her daughter, Sylvie Sator, who graciously allowed me to consult them in manuscript when I was writing *Revolution of the Mind.* They have since been published as André Breton, *Lettres à Simone Kahn, 1920–1960,* ed. Jean-Michel Goutier (Paris: Gallimard, 2016). Many of Kahn's own accounts were included in letters to her cousin Denise Lévy, which were published in Simone Breton, *Lettres à Denise Lévy.*

12. Crastre, quoted in Spector, *Surrealist Art and Writing,* 48 (trans. revised); Leiris, interview from 1968, quoted in Richardson and Fijalkowski, *Surrealism Against the Current,* 10.

13. For a discussion of this, see the introduction by Werner Spies to *La Révolution surréaliste,* exh. cat. (Paris: Centre Georges Pompidou, 2002), 26–27.

14. "Surrealist Situation of the Object" (1935), in *Manifestoes,* 260.

15. Breton, *Conversations,* 44 (trans. revised).

16. "Dada Manifesto 1918," in Tristan Tzara, *Seven Dada Manifestos and Lampisteries,* trans. Barbara Wright (London: John Calder, 1977), 4, 7, 12 (trans. revised).

17. Breton, *Conversations,* 40.

18. Ibid., 51. On relations between Dada and Surrealism, see Michel Sanouillet, *Dada in Paris,* trans. Sharmila Ganguly (Cambridge, Mass.: MIT Press, 2009).

19. Breton, *Conversations,* 42. The list of cities, incomplete (Hanover and Cologne are missing), is from Tzara's letterhead.

20. For an in-depth discussion of Surrealism as an international phenomenon, see D'Alessandro and Gale, *Surrealism Beyond Borders,* as well as *La planète affolée: Surréalisme, dispersion et influences, 1938–1947,* exh. cat. (Paris: Flammarion, 1986).

21. Extracts from the Congressional Record, speeches delivered on March 25 and August 16, 1949: https://theoria.art-zoo.com/from-the-congressional-record-george-dondero. Dondero is a human caricature, but Gertrude Stein, Henry Miller, and other Americans were also wary (see Polizzotti, *Revolution,* 384–85). Steven Harris specifies that "organized surrealist activity was renewed or established in the 1960s in Belgium, Brazil, Britain, Greece, the Netherlands, and the United States, and in the 1970s in Argentina, Australia, Canada, Iceland, and Spain; in the 1980s in Sweden; in the 1990s again in Britain and Brazil; and in the 2000s in Chile, Greece, and Turkey": "The Surrealist Movement since the 1940s," in Hopkins, *Companion to Dada and Surrealism,* 390. A contrary view was offered by Jean Schuster, a prominent postwar Surrealist and Breton's literary executor: "International Surrealism was a joke! It never really happened. There was the *illusion* in Surrealism of creating a great international movement. But there are only two countries in the world, outside of France, where one can speak of a Surrealist group: Belgium and England" (author interview with Jean Schuster, June 30, 1986).

22. Rafael Heliodoro Valle, "Diálogo con André Breton," *Universidad: Mensual de cultura popular* 29 (June 1938), 6; *British Surrealism,* exh. cat. (London: Dulwich Picture Gallery, 2020), 22.

23. Matt Stromberg, "Lisa Bowman's Exquisite Corpse Makes Connections Through the Mail," *Hyperallergic* (August 22, 2022), https://hyperallergic.com/754882/lisa-bowmans-exquisite-corpse-makes-connections-through-the-mail/.

24. Breton, *Conversations,* 238.

25. "Artistic Genesis and Perspective of Surrealism" (1941), in Breton, *Surrealism and Painting,* 70.

26. Max Ernst, *Beyond Painting* (1937), in Lippard, *Surrealists on Art,* 126–27. Ernst is referencing Lautréamont's oft-cited simile from *Maldoror and the Complete Works:* "Beautiful as the chance encounter of a sewing machine and an umbrella on a dissecting table."

27. Quoted in Guy Ducornet, *Le Punching-ball et la vache à lait: La Critique universitaire nord-américaine face au Surréalisme* (Angers: Actual / Deleatur, 1992), 22.

28. All quotations from *Surrealism and Painting,* see especially 1–6.

29. "Surrealist Comet" (1947), in Breton, *Free Rein,* 93. In 1960, the Surrealist poet Joyce Mansour, rejecting the notion of a "Surrealist way to paint," stated: "It is not the painting technique that is Surrealist but the painter: it is the painter's vision of life" (quoted in Spector, *Surrealist Art and Writing,* 250n11).

30. Michael Richardson, review of "Surrealism Beyond Borders," *Burlington Magazine* 164 (June 2022), 593–94.

31. Greenberg: "Surrealist Painting" (1944), in Clement Greenberg, *The Collected Essays and Criticism, Volume 1: Perceptions and Judgments, 1939–1944,* ed. John O'Brian (Chicago: University of Chicago Press, 1986), 226; Rubin, *Dada, Surrealism, and Their Heritage,* 15. See also Sandra Zalman, "The Canonisation of Surrealism in the United States," *Journal of Art Historiography* 19 (December 2018), https://arthistoriography.files.wordpress.com/2018/11/zalman.pdf.

TWO: TRANSFORMATION

1. Breton, *Manifesto,* 14. Shortly afterward, he cautions, "The marvelous is not the same in every period of history" (16).

2. "We want": André Breton, "Pourquoi je prends la direction de La Révolution surréaliste," *La Révolution surréaliste* 4 (July 15, 1925), 3; Césaire, quoted in Annette K. Joseph-Gabriel, "Haiti, Martinique, Cuba," in D'Alessandro and Gale, *Surrealism Beyond Borders,* 77. See

also Aragon, *Challenge to Painting* (1930): "The relationship born of the negation of the real by the marvelous is essentially of an ethical nature, and the marvelous is always the materialization of a moral symbol in violent opposition to the morality of the world from which it arises" (in Lippard, *Surrealists on Art,* 37).

3. Breton, *Nadja* (1928), 24; "The Uncanny," in Sigmund Freud, *Psychological Writings and Letters,* ed. Sander L. Gilman (New York: Continuum, 1995), 149–50.

4. Breton, *Mad Love* (1937), 8.

5. Miller, quoted in Matthew Beaumont, *The Walker: On Finding and Losing Yourself in the Modern City* (London: Verso, 2021), 6; "The New Spirit" (1922), in Breton, *Lost Steps,* 72–73.

6. Breton, *Mad Love,* 55–67.

7. "Lovely erector set": Aragon, *Anicet ou le Panorama, roman* (Paris: Gallimard, 1972), 29; "Mesopotamia": Aragon, *Paris Peasant,* 133.

8. Patrick Waldberg, "Jacques Hérold ou l'enfance de l'art" (1961), quoted in Georges Sebbag, *Memorabilia: Constellations inaperçues. Dada et Surrèalisme, 1916–1970* (Paris: Editions Cercle d'Art, 2010), 99.

9. "Sur certaines possibilités d'embellissement irrationnel d'une ville," *Le Surréalisme au service de la Révolution* 6 (May 15, 1933; hereafter *SASDLR*), 18–19.

10. "Five Dreams," in André Breton, *Earthlight,* trans. Bill Zavatsky and Zack Rogow (Boston: Black Widow Press, 2017), 57 (trans. revised).

11. ML Kejera, "21st Century Surrealism: The Omnipotence of Dream Memes," *New Inquiry* (February 10, 2022), https://thenewinquiry.com/21st-century-surrealism-the-omnipotence-of-dream-memes/; "psychoanalysis of reality": marginal note by Breton on the manuscript of his book *Communicating Vessels,* quoted in Breton, *Œuvres complètes,* vol. 2, ed. Marguerite Bonnet et al. (Paris: Gallimard / Bibliothèque de la Pléiade, 1992), 1353.

12. "Petrifying coincidence": Breton, *Nadja,* 19; "Surrealist aspiration": ibid., 74n. Breton first used the phrase "objective chance" in 1932,

quoting Engels: "Causality cannot be understood except as it is linked with the category of objective chance, a form of the manifestation of necessity": Breton, *Communicating Vessels,* 91–92.

13. Rosemont, *Inside the Magnetic Fields,* 103, 143.

14. "The Liquidation of Opium" (1925), trans. Helen Weaver, in Artaud, *Selected Writings,* 99.

15. Breton, *Manifesto,* 36.

16. Verlaine's original phrase is "Take eloquence and wring its neck!" See also Spector, *Surrealist Art and Writing,* 261n141. Eluard and Péret's proverbs were published as a pamphlet in 1925. Leiris's "Glossary" was published in installments in *La Révolution surréaliste* in 1925 and 1926.

17. This and the following quotations are from Breton, *Manifesto,* 21–23.

18. Breton, "Situation of Surrealism," 58. Cf. Jacqueline Chénieux-Gendron: "Surrealist thought is preoccupied with changing not the representation of the world but our understanding of it, an understanding that can only be expressed in the context of linguistic articulation": Introduction to Chénieux-Gendron, *"Il y aura une fois,"* 21.

19. Breton, *Manifesto,* 32.

20. Aragon, *Treatise on Style* (1928), 96; René Magritte, "Les Mots et les images," *La Révolution surréaliste* 12 (December 15, 1929), 32.

21. Marginal notes to *The Magnetic Fields,* in Breton, *Œuvres complètes,* vol. 1, ed. Marguerite Bonnet et al. (Paris: Gallimard / Bibliothèque de la Pléiade, 1988), 1130.

22. Breton and Soupault, *Magnetic Fields* (1920), 8, 25, 26, 57.

23. *Poésies,* in Lautréamont, *Maldoror,* 244.

24. "Stereotyped": Gershman, *Surrealist Revolution in France,* 70; "if you write": Aragon, *Treatise on Style,* 96, see also 94: "Rumor has it nowadays that it is enough to learn the trick, and that forthwith texts of great poetic interest will escape from the pen of every Tom, Dick, and Harry in an inexhaustible stream of diarrhea."

25. "Continual misfortune": "The Automatic Message" (1933), in Breton, *Break of Day*, 130; "vanity": "On Surrealism in Its Living Works" (1953), in *Manifestoes*, 297; "revealable portion": *Second Manifesto of Surrealism* (1929), ibid., 162n.

26. Breton, marginal notes to *Magnetic Fields*, 1155.

27. All quotations in this paragraph from Simone Kahn Breton to Denise Lévy, October 5 and 9, 1922, *Lettres à Denise Lévy*, 107–8 and 111. André Breton likely had these sessions in mind when he later wrote that Surrealism creates "a certain state of need." For an account of the sleep sessions, see Polizzotti, *Revolution*, 162–66.

28. René Crevel, "The Period of Sleeping-Fits," trans. Richard Thoma, *This Quarter*, Surrealist Number (September 1932), 185–86; "Sur Robert Desnos," in André Breton, *Perspective cavalière*, ed. Marguerite Bonnet (Paris: Gallimard, 1970), 170.

29. Jacqueline Chénieux-Gendron, "L'invention de l'automatisme, et du rêve comme discours," in *L'Invention du surréalisme: Des* Champs magnétiques *à* Nadja, exh. cat. (Paris: Bibliothèque Nationale de France, 2020), 64.

30. Breton, *Second Manifesto*, 123.

31. See Jacqueline Chénieux-Gendron, "Breton après Breton: Un 'rivage heureux pour notre pensée,'" in Myriam Blœdé, Pierre Caye, Jacqueline Chénieux-Gendron, and Martine Colin-Picon, eds., *La "Pensée-Breton": Art, magie, écriture chez André Breton* (Paris: L'Œil d'Or, 2021), 17, 20.

32. "Caught in the Act" (1949), in Breton, *Free Rein*, 128–29 (trans. revised). See also Breton's declaration from the *Manifesto:* "When someone ceases to feel, he should keep quiet" (8; trans. revised).

33. René Crevel, "The Patriotism of the Unconscious" (1931), in Ades and Richardson, *Surrealism Reader*, 115 (trans. revised).

34. "Derniers modes d'excitation intellectuelle pour l'été 1934," in Salvador Dalí, *Oui 2: L'Archangélisme scientifique* (Paris: Denoël / Gonthier, 1971), 40.

35. Salvador Dalí, "Nouvelles considérations générales sur le mécanisme du phénomène paranoïaque du point de vue surréaliste" (1933), in Chénieux-Gendron, *"Il y aura une fois,"* 191. Like Lacan, who early in his career had some involvement with the Surrealist group, Dalí considered paranoia an active psychic manifestation, versus what they saw as Freud's (and Breton's) "passive" view of it. My thanks to Christopher Sawyer-Lauçanno for pointing this out.

36. "Hand-painted color photographs": Dalí, "Derniers modes," 40; "insipid and imbecilic": Dalí, *Mythe tragique* (originally published 1963), 51, 40.

37. Nadeau, *History of Surrealism,* 188.

38. René Crevel, *Dalí ou l'anti-obscurantisme* (Paris: Editions Surréalistes, 1931), 23. Oppenheim didn't care to be labeled a Surrealist and considered her cup and saucer a minor work; the title *Breakfast in Fur* was suggested by Breton (see Spector, *Surrealist Art and Writing,* 293n173). A thorough study of Surrealist objects can be found in Ottinger, *Dictionnaire de l'objet surréaliste.*

39. "Rêve-objet" (1935), in Breton, *Œuvres complètes,* vol. 2, 558–59.

40. Quoted in Judith Young Mallin, "Eileen Agar," in Caws, Kuenzli, and Raaberg, *Surrealism and Women,* 225. By the 1930s, Breton, worried about the profusion of counterfeit Surrealist objects, was positing that the genuine article ought to be stamped for authenticity ("Surrealist Situation of the Object," 257).

41. Jonathan Jones, review of "Objects of Desire," *Guardian* (October 12, 2022), https://www.theguardian.com/artanddesign/2022/oct/12/objects-of-desire-review-surreal-lobster-phones-and-a-seaside-sleazorama.

42. Breton, "Surrealist Situation of the Object," 261.

43. "Precipitate": "Surrealist Exhibition of Objects" (1936), in Breton, *Surrealism and Painting,* 283; "objectification:" ibid., 277. See also Breton, "Surrealist Situation of the Object," 262.

1. Jonathan Lethem, "The Ecstasy of Influence: A Plagiarism," *Harper's* (February 2007), https://harpers.org/archive/2007/02/the-ecstasy-of-influence/. Similarly, the subtitle of this chapter was appropriated from the 1993 book by historian Eric Lott, via Bob Dylan's appropriation of it for his eponymous 2001 album.

2. *Poésies,* in Lautréamont, *Maldoror,* 240.

3. In 1942, Breton wrote of "the New Guineans whose art has always captivated certain of us much more than Egyptian or Roman art" ("Prolegomena to a Third Surrealist Manifesto or Not," in *Manifestoes,* 284). For a fuller discussion, see Mark Polizzotti, "Breton's Smartphone: Surrealism in the Digital Age," *Catamaran* 28 (spring 2020), 135–39.

4. "Produce passion": Breton, *Mad Love,* 8; "justify": Breton, *Conversations,* 202; "very deep affinities": ibid., 193. On the collective nature of Oceanic art, see Maia Nuku, "Power and Agency in Oceanic Art," in D'Alessandro and Gale, *Surrealism Beyond Borders,* 184–85. See also Blachère, *Totems d'André Breton,* and Florence Duchemin-Pelletier, "Surréalisme et art inuit: La fascination du Grand Nord," *Journal of Surrealism and the Americas* 2, no. 1 (2008), 64–94, esp. 72–73. Breton, Ernst, Claude Lévi-Strauss, and others found a number of these objects during their wartime exile in New York at the Julius Carlebach Gallery at 937 Third Avenue; their collecting was encouraged by the fact that, at the time, the items were little prized and comparatively inexpensive. However, according to Duchemin-Pelletier (69–70), they had already become aware of, and acquired, works from the Great Northwest in the 1930s, clued in by exhibitions at the Musée du Trocadéro and the Galerie Charles Ratton.

5. Hayden Herrera, *Frida: A Biography of Frida Kahlo* (New York: Harper and Row, 1983), 230. See also Eileen Agar's widely reproduced comment: "One day I was an artist exploring personal combinations of form and content, and the next I was calmly informed I was a Surrealist!" Man Ray gleefully reported to Gertrude Stein a similar, and

similarly vain, attempt on Breton's part to persuade Matisse that *he* was a Surrealist: Neil Baldwin, *Man Ray: American Artist* (New York: Clarkson N. Potter, 1988), 125.

6. Hal Foster, "At Tate Modern: Surrealism Beyond Borders," *London Review of Books* (May 26, 2022), https://www.lrb.co.uk/the-paper/v44/n10/hal-foster/at-tate-modern.

7. Author interview with Claude Lévi-Strauss, February 21, 1989, in Polizzotti, *Revolution,* 455.

8. Elza Adamowicz, *The Eye of the Poet: André Breton and the Visual Arts* (London: Reaktion Books, 2022), 190.

9. Katherine Dwyer, "France's New Nazis: The Resistible Rise of Jean-Marie LePen," *International Socialist Review* 2 (fall 1997), https://isreview.org/issues/02/LePen/.

10. "Racist concepts": Daniel Bénédite, *La Filière marseillaise: Un chemin vers la liberté sous l'Occupation* (Paris: Clancier Guénaud, 1984), 124–25; "friends of color": "Speech to Young Haitian Poets," trans. Stephen Schwartz, in Breton, *What Is Surrealism?,* 260 (trans. revised). See also Joseph-Gabriel, "Haiti, Martinique, Cuba," 74–79, and Polizzotti, *Revolution,* 442.

11. "Surrealism is allied": Breton, *Conversations,* 193; "let's not exaggerate": ibid., 201; "helped create": Roger Gaillard, "André Breton et nous," quoted in Polizzotti, *Revolution,* 480; "had no intention": quoted in Lewis, *Politics of Surrealism,* 164.

12. Grace Byron, "A Cynic's Fairy Tale: On the Met's 'Surrealism Beyond Borders,'" *Observer* (January 10, 2022), https://observer.com/2022/01/a-cynics-fairy-tale-on-the-mets-surrealism-beyond-borders/.

13. Pierre, *Investigating Sex,* 57.

14. "Contact with Jews": author interview with Edouard Roditi, June 11, 1987; "intellectual filth": "Against Céline" (June 22, 1957; letter unpublished), in Richardson and Fijalkowski, *Surrealism Against the Current,* 163–64. For a detailed discussion of the incompatibility of

Surrealism and Judaism, see Gideon Ofrat, "Why Is There No Jewish Surrealism?," *Shofar* 32, no. 3 (Spring 2014), 102–19. Among other reasons, Ofrat notes wryly that "the surrealist closes his or her eyes. . . . A Jew will close only one eye, keeping a weather eye open to see where the next pogrom may come from" (107). The controversy surrounding Céline was reignited in 2022 by the discovery of his unknown manuscripts and reissues of his vicious wartime pamphlets: see Alice Kaplan, "The Master of Blame," *New York Review of Books* (July 21, 2022).

15. "The Mongols": "Revolution First and Always!," in Richardson and Fijalkowski, *Surrealism Against the Current,* 96; "the oppressors and the oppressed": Paul Eluard, "Yen-Bay," *SASDLR* 1 (July 1930), 8.

16. "Murderous Humanitarianism," trans. Samuel Beckett, in Richardson and Fijalkowski, *Surrealism Against the Current,* 190–91. See also Partha Mitter, "Surrealism and the Global Colonial Order," in D'Alessandro and Gale, *Surrealism Beyond Borders,* 212–14.

17. Aimé Césaire, *Return to My Native Land,* trans. John Berger and Anna Bostock (Brooklyn: Archipelago Books, 2013), 9.

18. "Greatest lyrical monument": "A Great Black Poet: Aimé Césaire" (1943), trans. Dale Tomich, in Breton, *What Is Surrealism?,* 232; "crucial and decisive": quoted in Virmaux and Virmaux, *Breton qui êtes-vous?,* 103–4; "a revelation": quoted in Rosemont, *Inside the Magnetic Fields,* 164; "resound everywhere": quoted in D'Alessandro and Gale, *Surrealism Beyond Borders,* 31.

19. D'Alessandro and Gale, *Surrealism Beyond Borders,* 16, see also 17–31. Breton's impressions of his stay can be found in André Breton, *Martinique: Snake Charmer* (1948; in collaboration with André Masson), trans. David W. Seaman (Austin: University of Texas Press, 2008).

20. Ménil's critique of Senghor (René Ménil, "The Passage from Poetry to Philosophy," in Ades and Richardson, *Surrealism Reader,* 151, 158) was partly in response to Senghor's contention that "Negro-African surrealism is mystical" while "European Surrealism is empirical": see

L. S. Senghor, *Liberté 1* (1964), quoted in Jean-Claude Michel, *The Black Surrealists* (New York: Peter Lang, 2000), 114.

21. "A weapon": quoted in Ara H. Merjian, "Surrealism and Politics," *ARTnews* (April 7, 2022), https://www.artnews.com/art-in-america/features/surrealism-global-politics-1234624356/; "as a means": quoted in D'Alessandro and Gale, *Surrealism Beyond Borders,* 20; "quivering of her ovaries": Annie Le Brun, "A Creolism Sewn with White Thread," in Ades and Richardson, *Surrealism Reader,* 160–72. See also Spector, *Surrealist Art and Writing,* 189–90; Yasmina Price, "Lambasting Reality," *Art in America* (April 28, 2022), https://www.artnews.com/art-in-america/features/afrosurrealism-film-jatovia-gary-christopher-harris-madline-hunt-ehrlich-nuotama-bodomo-1234626904; Lori Cole, "Légitime défense: From Communism and Surrealism to Caribbean Self-Definition," *Journal of Surrealism and the Americas* 4, no. 1 (2010), 15–30; "Négritude," *Stanford Encyclopedia of Philosophy* (May 24, 2010), https://plato.stanford.edu/entries/negritude/#NegRevNeg.

22. Ayoola Solarin, "The Importance of Afrosurrealism in 2020," *i-D* (November 10, 2020), https://i-d.vice.com/en_uk/article/dy8v5w/an-ode-to-afrosurrealism-photography-exhibition-by-adama-jalloh-and-hamed-maiye/.

23. D. Scot Miller, "Afrosurreal Manifesto: Black Is the New black—a 21st-Century Manifesto," https://muse.jhu.edu/article/525948/pdf. Miller coined the term "Afrosurrealism" after Amiri Baraka's 1974 coinage "Afrosurreal Expressionism."

24. "Afro-Surrealism," https://en.wikipedia.org/wiki/Afro-Surrealism, accessed November 13, 2020; this point, in a paragraph about the cinematographer Arthur Jafa, was removed in 2021.

25. Rosemont, *Inside the Magnetic Fields,* 110–11; Joanna Pawlik, "Ted Joans: Overseas Surrealism," in D'Alessandro and Gale, *Surrealism Beyond Borders,* 160–63.

26. Quoted in Pawlik, "Ted Joans," 163.

27. Quoted in Rosemont, *Inside the Magnetic Fields,* 110.

28. "Advertisement for heaven": Breton to Aragon, April 13, 1919, quoted in Aragon, "Lautréamont et nous," *Les Lettres françaises* (June 8, 1967), 7; "striking enough": Breton, marginal notes to *Magnetic Fields,* 1152.

29. Guillaume Apollinaire, *L'Esprit nouveau et les poètes* (Paris: Altamira, 1994), 20 (lecture delivered in November 1917).

30. Breton to Aragon, April 17–18, 1919, in Aragon, "Lautréamont et nous," 7.

31. Aragon, *Aragon parle avec Dominique Arban* (Paris: Seghers, 1968), 134.

32. Tzara, "Dada Manifesto 1918," 8 (trans. revised). Breton's "PSTT" was published in *Clair de terre* (1923) and Aragon's "Suicide" in *Le Mouvement perpétuel* (1926).

33. See Elliott H. King, "Surrealism and Counterculture," in Hopkins, *Companion to Dada and Surrealism,* 416–30.

34. Breton, *Manifesto,* 37 (trans. revised). See also his claim that "each of us has within himself the potential of an orator: multicolored loincloths, glass trinkets of words" (ibid., 31).

35. Sebbag, *Surréalisme,* 9, 34; "Du manifeste surréaliste," in *Manifestes DADA surréalistes,* ed. Georges Sebbag (Paris: Jean-Michel Place, 2005), 154. As of this writing, TikTok has, in fact, become a major generator of Surrealist-inspired videos: https://www.pastemagazine.com/comedy/tik-tok-comedy/.

36. For a full account, see Polizzotti, *Revolution,* 545–46. Such performances nonetheless *were* carried forward, notably by conceptual artists such as Chris Burden, who had himself shot in the shoulder before an audience (*Shoot,* 1971). Robert Hughes ("The Decline and Fall of the Avant-Garde," *Time* [December 18, 1972], 111) also reported that in 1969, the Austrian artist Rudolf Schwarzkogler amputated his own penis inch by inch until it finally caused his death, but this has since been debunked.

1. "Clearly," in Breton, *Lost Steps,* 81.

2. Breton, *Second Manifesto,* 123; Durozoi, *History of the Surrealist Movement,* 647.

3. The Surrealists' transcript of the Barrès trial, which took up the entire issue, was published in *Littérature* 20 (August 1921). See also *L'Affaire Barrès,* ed. Marguerite Bonnet (Paris: José Corti / Actual, 1987). Another Surrealist exercise in cancellation was a dual list from 1931 headlined "Read / Don't Read," the "Don't Reads" being the longer of the two and ending in "etc., etc., etc."

4. Quotations from *A Corpse* and the "Open Letter" in Nadeau, *History of Surrealism,* 235, 238.

5. "Open the Prisons! Disband the Army!," trans. Richard Howard, in Breton, *What Is Surrealism?,* 316 (trans. revised); originally published in *La Révolution surréaliste* 2 (January 15, 1925).

6. Breton, *Second Manifesto,* 125. See also Jonathan P. Eburne, "Crime / Insurrection," in Hopkins, *Companion to Dada and Surrealism,* 258–69.

7. John Schoneboom, "Surreality, Propaganda, and Wile E. Coyote," *WhoWhatWhy* (November 29, 2022), https://whowhatwhy.org/culture/surreality-propaganda-and-wile-e-coyote/.

8. "Sade wished to give back": Paul Eluard, "Poetic Evidence," trans. George Reavey, in *Surrealism,* ed. Herbert Read (1936; repr., London: Faber and Faber, 1971), 177; "let us feel": *Philosophy in the Bedroom,* in Marquis de Sade, *Justine, Philosophy in the Bedroom, and Other Writings,* trans. Richard Seaver and Austryn Wainhouse (New York: Grove Press, 1965), 217. See also Paul Eluard, "D. A. F. de Sade, écrivain fantastique et révolutionnaire," in *La Révolution surréaliste* 8 (December 1, 1926), 8–9, and Neil Cox, "Desire Bound: Violence, Body, Machine," in Hopkins, *Companion to Dada and Surrealism,* 334–51.

9. "Free development": "Letter to the Head Doctors of Insane Asylums," in Richardson and Fijalkowski, *Surrealism Against the Current,*

141 (originally published in *La Révolution surréaliste* 3 [April 15, 1925]); "all confinements": Breton, *Nadja,* 141; "all men are equal": Salvador Dalí, "Declaration of the Independence of the Imagination and the Rights of Man to His Own Madness" (written for his pavilion at the 1939 World's Fair in New York), https://www.artic.edu/dali-manifesto.

10. Quoted in Ducornet, *Punching-ball,* 145.

11. Aragon, *La Révolution surréaliste* 4 (here again following Rimbaud), quoted in Spector, *Surrealist Art and Writing,* 86; Thirion, quoted in Lewis, *Politics,* 81. Pushing the spirit of subversion, in 2022 a screed sponsored by the English Surrealist-oriented group around Safety Propaganda / Morbid Books bucked the trend by calling for an end to "the passive nihilism of the 'quiet quitter'" and a return to basic competence as a means of active resistance: Lev Parker, "Be Competent," https://safetypropaganda.substack.com/p/edgelord-4-be-competent-by-lev-parker?mc_cid=9463401e88&mc_eid=2b92a76b4a.

12. Breton, *Nadja,* 59–60.

13. Abigail Susik, "Down with Work!," *Idler* 84 (May–June 2022), 38. For a fuller treatment, see Abigail Susik, *Surrealist Sabotage and the War on Work* (Manchester: Manchester University Press, 2021).

14. The phrase is from Breton's poem "Il n'y pas à sortir de là."

15. Quoted in Marko Ristić, "Humour as a Moral Attitude," in Ades and Richardson, *Surrealism Reader,* 198. In a blackly humorous twist, Popević renounced Surrealism after World War II to become Tito's right-hand man.

16. Breton, *Anthology of Black Humor,* xvi, xix.

17. "The enthusiasms": Vaché to Breton, April 29, 1917, in Vaché, *Lettres de guerre,* 231; "art doesn't exist": Vaché to Breton, August 18, 1918, ibid., 291–92. Various English translations are available of Vaché's letters to Breton, none satisfactory.

18. Breton, *Conversations,* 18.

19. "Desertion within oneself": Breton, *Anthology of Black Humor,* 293; "object to being killed": Vaché to Breton, May 9, 1918, Vaché,

Lettres de guerre, 316; "it is a sensation": Vaché to Breton, April 29, 1917, ibid., 231. Writing this in the context of the Covid-19 pandemic, I'm struck by how much Vaché's "joyless pointlessness" sounds like the global syndrome of "languishing"—hardly humorous, but all too topical.

20. "Absolutely savage": Breton, marginal notes to *Magnetic Fields,* 1130 (relating that he and Soupault would burst out laughing when they read what they had written); "charged": "As in a Wood," in Breton, *Free Rein,* 236.

21. Breton, *Manifesto,* 39. See also David Hopkins, *Dark Toys: Surrealism and Culture of Childhood* (New Haven: Yale University Press, 2021), and Alastair Brotchie and Mel Gooding, eds., *Surrealist Games* (Boston: Shambhala, 1993).

22. "Fragile friendships": Robert Benayoun, *Le Rire des surréalistes* (Paris: La Bougie du Sapeur, 1988), 81; "within any other": "L'un dans l'autre" (1954), in Breton, *Perspective cavalière,* 53. On the Marseilles Game see Tessel M. Bauduin, *Surrealism and the Occult: Occultism and Western Esotericism in the Work and Movement of André Breton* (Amsterdam: Amsterdam University Press, 2014), 138–42, and Bernard Noël, *Marseille–New York, 1940–1945: Une liaison surréaliste* (Marseille: André Dimanche, 1985).

23. Simone [Breton] Collinet, "The Exquisite Corpse," in *Le Cadavre exquis, son exaltation,* exh. cat. (Milan: Galleria Schwarz, 1975), 30.

24. "Follows such games": Aragon, *Paris Peasant,* 131; "initiation rite": Jacques Baron, *L'An 1 du surréalisme* (Paris: Denoël, 1969), 81; "sheer play": Johan Huizinga, *Homo Ludens: A Study of the Play-Element in Culture* (London: Routledge and Kegan Paul, 1949), 20, also 9–13. See also Gershman, *Surrealist Revolution in France,* 9–10.

25. "Dissident ends": Tessel M. Bauduin, "De Schone Zakdoek," in D'Alessandro and Gale, *Surrealism Beyond Borders,* 191: the author is specifically referring to the Schone Zakdoek ("Clean Kerchief") group in the Netherlands during World War II; "respect to it": Jean-Louis Bédouin, *Vingt ans du surréalisme, 1939–1959* (Paris: Denoël, 1961), 27.

1. Breton, *Manifesto,* 44n.

2. Breton, "On Surrealism in Its Living Works," 301–2 (trans. revised).

3. Sebbag, *Surréalisme,* 103.

4. Breton, *Arcanum 17* (1945), 114–15. See also Gauthier, *Surréalisme et sexualité,* 201, and Thirion, *Revolutionaries Without Revolution,* 99.

5. Marcel Duhamel, *Raconte pas ta vie* (Paris: Mercure de France, 1972), 252; Breton's quotations are from Pierre, *Investigating Sex,* passim, see esp. 13, 117. The first two sessions were originally published in *La Révolution surréaliste* 11 (March 15, 1928), 32–40, with the unrealized promise "to be continued."

6. Pierre, *Investigating Sex,* 5; see also 27–28.

7. Nora Mitrani, "Une solitude enchantée," in Chénieux-Gendron, *"Il y aura une fois,"* 140–43, see also 24.

8. "Stank of bourgeois": Maxime Alexandre, *Mémoires d'un surréaliste* (Paris: La Jeune Parque, 1968), 209; "who dared maintain": Breton, *Conversations,* 131. Dalí's "Rêverie" was published in *SASDLR* 4 (December 1931). As early as 1920, in "Le Démon du foyer," Breton and Aragon called for women to rebel against marriage (Breton, *Œuvres complètes,* vol. 1, 407).

9. Clara Zetkin, "Lenin on the *Women's Question,*" https://www.marxists.org/archive/zetkin/1920/lenin/zetkin1.htm; Gauthier, *Surréalisme et sexualité,* 43–50; sexual positions: Pierre, *Investigating Sex,* 29. Lenin was nonetheless more progressive than his successor: legislation passed in the early days of the Soviet regime, such as legalized divorce and free access to abortion, were later reversed under Stalin.

10. "Sometimes repressed": Breton, *Communicating Vessels,* 68 (trans. revised); "repressive reality": Herbert Marcuse, *Eros and Civilization: A Philosophical Inquiry into Freud* (1955; repr., Boston: Beacon Press,

1974), 95; "side of Eros": Gauthier, *Surréalisme et sexualité,* 283. See also Alyce Mahon, *Surrealism and the Politics of Eros,* esp. 15–17.

11. "The problem of woman": Breton, *Second Manifesto,* 180; "may we be ruled": Breton, *Arcanum 17,* 51, 61 (trans. revised). Breton is no doubt channeling Rimbaud's famous "seer letter" to Paul Demeny of May 15, 1871: "When the endless serfdom of woman is toppled, when she can live for herself and by herself . . . she too will be a poet! Woman will find the unknown! Will the worlds of her ideas differ from ours?" See Arthur Rimbaud, *The Drunken Boat: Selected Writings,* ed. and trans. Mark Polizzotti (New York: New York Review Books, 2022), 231.

12. "Permitted not required": Sacha Llewellyn, "'Permitted Not Required': British Women Surrealists," in *British Surrealism,* 123; "bullshit role": author interview with Leonora Carrington, April 25, 1986.

13. "A companion": "The Disdainful Confession," in Breton, *Lost Steps,* 4, in which he specifies that he left his door "wide open" in hopes of encouraging this event; "female traits": Breton, *Conversations,* 106.

14. Favorite color: Charles Duits, *Breton a-t-il dit passe* (1969; rev. ed., Paris: Maurice Nadeau, 1991), 104; Tanning, quoted in Chadwick, *Women Artists and the Surrealist Movement,* 11; Agar, quoted in Caws, Kuenzli, and Raaberg, *Surrealism and Women,* 219; Colquhoun: *British Surrealism,* 86.

15. Gwen Raaberg, "The Problematics of Women and Surrealism," in Caws, Kuenzli, and Raaberg, *Surrealism and Women,* 2–3.

16. Breton, *Arcanum 17,* 61 (my emphasis).

17. "The only motive": Breton, *Mad Love,* 88; "in total freedom": *The Air of the Water* (1934), in Breton, *Earthlight,* 287.

18. Simone de Beauvoir, *The Second Sex,* trans. Constance Borde and Sheila Malovany-Chevallier (New York: Vintage, 2011); Gauthier, *Surréalisme et sexualité,* 196, see also 157, 204, et passim; Breton, *Arcanum 17,* 38 (note the "of course").

19. Breton, *Mad Love,* 93.

20. "Fixed forever": Gauthier, *Surréalisme et sexualité,* 79; "she has the shape": "A Woman in Love," in Paul Eluard, *Capital of Pain,* trans. Mary Ann Caws, Patricia Terry, and Nancy Kline (Boston: Black Widow Press, 2006), 89.

21. "Free Union," in Breton, *Earthlight,* 151, 155.

22. Georges Bataille, *Story of the Eye* (1928), trans. Joachim Neugroschel (New York: Penguin Classics, 2001), 67.

23. Breton, *Arcanum 17,* 64–65.

24. Benjamin Péret, *Anthologie de l'amour sublime* (1956), quoted in Gauthier, *Surréalisme et sexualité,* 109.

25. "It is so sweet": Sade, *Philosophy in the Bedroom,* 247; "I was an androgyne": "Down Below," in Leonora Carrington, *House of Fear* (New York: Dutton, 1988), 195. See Gauthier, *Surréalisme et sexualité,* 272–73: "For an authentically revolutionary movement, it's not about systematically inverting [gender] roles, which would make no sense, but of blurring them."

26. Rudolf E. Kuenzli, "Surrealism and Misogyny," in Caws, Kuenzli, and Raaberg, *Surrealism and Women,* 24. See also Mary Ann Caws, "Ladies Shot and Painted: Female Embodiment in Surrealist Art," in Susan Rubin Suleiman, ed., *The Female Body in Western Culture: Contemporary Perspectives* (Cambridge, Mass.: Harvard University Press, 1986), 262–87.

27. Quoted in Ducornet, *Punching-ball,* 89. Cf. Mahon: "When male Surrealist artists focus on the female body in their paintings or installations, they celebrate the erotic power of the female body and the uncanny power of the feminine in us all": *Surrealism and the Politics of Eros,* 19.

28. "For us women": quoted in Philomena Epps, "A Slew of Shows Celebrates Surrealist Women," *Frieze* (September 17, 2020), https://www.frieze.com/article/slew-shows-celebrates-surrealist-women; Rosemont, *Inside the Magnetic Fields,* 162–63. See also Katharine Conley's assertion from 2011: "No critic can claim any longer that women

did not play a significant role in what I have called the surrealist conversation, namely the launch, exchange, and constant adjustment and reformulation of circulating ideas, images, metaphors, and jokes of the sort typical of a group conversation conducted in a café or over a dinner table": "Women in the Surrealist Conversation," *Journal of Surrealism and the Americas* 5, nos. 1–2 (2011), i.

29. Quoted in Llewellyn, "'Permitted Not Required,'" 127. Cf. Llewellyn's observation that the British women Surrealists "mapped out their own autonomous identities . . . to produce radical works centered on the female condition" (ibid.).

30. Nancy Joyce Peters, "Women and Surrealism," in Rosemont, *Surrealist Women,* 459.

31. Carrington, *House of Fear,* 5.

32. Both quotations: Ayanna Dozier, "Women Artists Are Painting Fresh Visions of Sex with a Surrealistic Twist," *Artsy* (August 11, 2022), https://www.artsy.net/article/artsy-editorial-women-artists-painting-fresh-visions-sex-surrealistic-twist.

33. "Qualifications or goals": Dorothea Tanning, "Statement," in Caws, Kuenzli, and Raaberg, *Surrealism and Women,* 228; "artist or poet": Robert J. Belton, "Androgyny: Interview with Meret Oppenheim," ibid., 66.

SIX: DISRUPTION

1. Breton, *Conversations,* 225.

2. Eburne, "Crime / Insurrection," 262. See also Raymond Spiteri, "Surrealism and the Question of Politics, 1925–1939," in Hopkins, *Companion to Dada and Surrealism,* 110–30.

3. Breton, *Conversations,* 172.

4. "Primacy of passion": Breton, *Conversations,* 210; "Surrealist illumination": quoted in Nadeau, *History of Surrealism,* 105n. There were exceptions, of course: The Prague group was more directly engaged

with politics, even if its own relations with the Czech Communists were not always easy. As noted earlier, Léopold Senghor became president of Senegal, and Aimé Césaire served as deputy for Martinique to the French National Assembly. Even within the Paris group, there were figures such as André Thirion, who became a minister in the Gaullist cabinet after World War II.

5. "Sweat with him": *Aragon parle,* 87–88; "repellent": unpublished diary entry, December 28, 1920, Breton, *Œuvres complètes,* vol. 1, 614–15.

6. Quotations from *A Corpse* and Aragon's rebuttal to Bernier: Nadeau, *History of Surrealism,* 100–101 (trans. revised). For an in-depth account in French of the Surrealists' political engagements, see Carole Reynaud Paligot, *Parcours politique des surréalistes, 1919–1969* (Paris: CNRS Editions, 1995).

7. "Revolution First and Always!," in Richardson and Fijalkowski, *Surrealism Against the Current,* 95; Julien Gracq, "Des rendez-vous décevants avec l'histoire," in Marie-Claire Dumas, ed., *André Breton en perspective cavalière* (Paris: Gallimard, 1996), 17.

8. "Leon Trotsky's 'Lenin,'" trans. Stephen Schwartz, in Breton, *What Is Surrealism?*, 30 (trans. slightly revised). Originally published in *La Révolution surréaliste* 5 (October 15, 1925).

9. Both quotations: Breton, *Conversations,* 93.

10. "Give a damn": *Adhérer au Parti communiste?*, ed. Marguerite Bonnet, vol. 3, *Archives du surréalisme* (Paris: Gallimard, 1992), 24–25; "toilet-paper": "On the Alfred Jarry Theater" (note from November 1926), in Artaud, *Selected Writings,* 161; "In Total Darkness, or the Surrealist Bluff" (1927), ibid., 139–40.

11. Pierre Naville, *La Révolution et les intellectuels* (1926; repr., Paris: Gallimard, 1975), 58, 65, 86–87. See also Polizzotti, *Revolution,* esp. 230–31, 242.

12. "In Self-Defense" (1926), in Breton, *Break of Day,* 34.

13. Ibid., 23 and 23n.

14. Lewis, *Politics,* 173, see also 49. Desnos tried to argue that Breton's original definition of Surrealism as "psychic automatism . . . in the absence of any control exercised by reason" was "perfectly compatible with the revolution" because Breton meant *bourgeois* reason: see "Le sens révolutionnaire du surréalisme" (1925), in Robert Desnos, *Nouvelles Hébrides et autres textes, 1922–1930,* ed. Marie-Claire Dumas (Paris: Gallimard, 1978), 233.

15. "Needed intellectuals": Lewis, *Politics,* 76; "if you're a Marxist": Breton, *Second Manifesto,* 142; "nothing seemed more": Breton, *Conversations,* 100.

16. Both quotations: Lewis, *Politics,* 121–22.

17. Michel Leiris, *The Cardinal Point,* trans. Terry Hale, in *The Automatic Muse* (London: Atlas Press, 1994), 93. Raymond Spiteri ("Surrealism and the Question of Politics," 111) nonetheless points out that in positing a Surrealist solution to the "principal problems of life" in the *Manifesto,* Breton was already situating Surrealism on a political footing.

18. My thanks to Roger Reeves for drawing my attention to these lines.

19. Aragon, "Déclaration" (November 1925), *Vers l'action politique,* ed. Marguerite Bonnet, vol. 2, *Archives du surréalisme* (Paris: Gallimard, 1988), 103; Lewis, *Politics,* 47; Luis Buñuel, *My Last Sigh,* trans. Abigail Israel (New York: Alfred A. Knopf, 1983), 138.

20. Lewis, *Politics,* 54.

21. Aragon, "Pour un réalisme socialiste" (1935), quoted in Lewis, *Politics,* 97. For an account of the "Aragon affair," see Polizzotti, *Revolution,* 318–21, 332–37. Breton, recalling the breakup years later, admitted that the memory of it was "like a wound being reopened every time" (*Conversations,* 172).

22. "One of our first duties": "Political Position of Surrealism," in *Manifestoes,* 240; "a work is revolutionary": quoted in Sebbag, *Surréalisme,* 78; "mental extermination": "Of 'Socialist Realism' as a Means

of Mental Extermination," in Breton, *Free Rein,* 274. The irony is that, in this regard, the Soviet position did not substantially differ from that of the Nazis, who at the same time were co-opting art in support of *their* position and deriding the same "degenerate" avant-garde that was infuriating the Communists.

23. Ilya Ehrenburg, "The Surrealists," trans. Samuel Putnam, *Partisan Review* (October–November 1935), 11–16. Article originally written in July 1933 and included in Ehrenburg's *Duhamel, Gide, Malraux, Mauriac, Morand, Romains, Unamuno vus par un écrivain d'U.R.S.S.* (Paris: Gallimard, 1934), which is where Breton likely came across it.

24. "Speech to the Congress of Writers" (1935), in *Manifestoes,* 235, 240–41 (trans. revised). On the Congress, see "Having Congress: The Shame of the Thirties," in Roger Shattuck, *The Innocent Eye: On Modern Literature and the Arts* (Boston: MFA Publications, 2003), 3–31, and Herbert Lottman, *The Left Bank: Writers, Artists and Politics from the Popular Front to the Cold War* (Boston: Houghton Mifflin, 1982), 83–98.

25. "To be forced": "On the Time When the Surrealists Were Right," in *Manifestoes,* 248, 253; "finally toppled": Breton, *Conversations,* 139.

26. André Breton, "Declaration: 'The Truth about the Moscow Trials,'" in Richardson and Fijalkowski, *Surrealism Against the Current,* 118.

27. Quoted in Lewis, *Politics,* 146.

28. André Breton and Diego Rivera [*sic*], "Manifesto: Towards a Free Revolutionary Art," trans. Dwight Macdonald, *Partisan Review* 6, no. 1 (fall 1938), 53; the manifesto was cosigned by Rivera owing to the conditions of Trotsky's asylum in Mexico. For a fuller account, see Polizzotti, *Revolution,* 407–19.

29. Breton, *Conversations,* 151.

30. Breton, "Situation of Surrealism," 56, 61.

31. *New York Times* (November 25, 1945), quoted in Meryle Secrest, *Salvador Dalí* (New York: E. P. Dutton, 1986), 191.

32. Magritte to Breton, June 24, 1946, https://www.andrebreton.fr/en/work/56600101000930.

33. Gershman, *Surrealist Revolution in France,* 116.

34. "The Lamp in the Clock" (1948), in Breton, *Free Rein,* 108.

35. Gershman, *Surrealist Revolution in France,* 134.

SEVEN: REVOLUTION

1. "True element": Breton, "Disdainful Confession," 4; "at the students' disposal": "Pas de Pasteurs pour cette Rage!" (May 5, 1968), in José Pierre, ed., *Tracts surréalistes et déclarations collectives,* vol. 2, *1940–1969* (Paris: Eric Losfeld / Le Terrain Vague, 1982), 276.

2. All quotations: author interview with Claude Courtot, June 24, 1986. Jean Schuster, too, termed the May revolt "a great contribution to the dissolution of the group": conversation with author, March 1, 1988.

3. Jean Schuster, "The Fourth Canto," trans. Peter Wood, in Richardson and Fijalkowski, *Surrealism Against the Current,* 200–201; the article was originally published in *Le Monde* (October 4, 1969). See also Rosemont, *Inside the Magnetic Fields,* 168. Steven Harris argues that Surrealism "continues today [2016] in organized collective activity in Argentina, Brazil, Britain, Canada, Chile, the Czech and Slovak Republics, France, Greece, the Netherlands, Portugal, Spain, Sweden, and the United States": Harris, "The Surrealist Movement since the 1940s," 385.

4. Breton, "Prolegomena," 289 (trans. revised).

5. John Ashbery, "Growing up Surreal," *Art News* (May 1968), 41. See also this reflection of Ashbery's from four years earlier: "Surrealism has become part of our daily lives: its effects can be seen everywhere, in the work of artists and writers who have no connection with the movement, in movies, interior decoration and popular speech. A degradation? Perhaps. But it is difficult to impose limitations on the unconscious, which has a habit of turning up in unlikely places":

"In the Surrealist Tradition," in John Ashbery, *Reported Sightings: Art Chronicles 1957–1987,* ed. David Bergman (New York: Alfred A. Knopf, 1989), 4.

6. Guy Debord, "Contribution to the Debate 'Is Surrealism Dead or Alive?' " (1958), in Tom McDonough, ed., *Guy Debord and the Situationist International: Texts and Documents* (Cambridge, Mass.: MIT Press, 2004), 68.

7. Philippe Audoin, "Festival Mood" (1965), in Ades and Richardson, *Surrealism Reader,* 237–38. Audoin is leaning in part on James Burnham's *The Managerial Revolution* (1941). Note the ironic reversal of the Surrealist attitude toward advertising.

8. Schoneboom, "Surreality, Propaganda, and Wile E. Coyote."

9. Lewis, *Politics,* 173.

10. Breton, *Conversations,* 172.

11. "A Swimmer Between Two Words," trans. Robert Hurley, in Michel Foucault, *Aesthetics, Method, and Epistemology,* ed. James D. Faubion (New York: New Press, 1998), 174.

12. Gracq, "Des rendez-vous décevants," 22–23.

13. Rex Weiner, *High Times* (April 1977), https://hightimes.com/culture/flashback-friday-surrealism/.

14. Pierre, *Tracts,* vol. 2, 300.

15. Robert Storr, "Past Imperfect, Present Conditional," in *Max Ernst: A Retrospective,* ed. Werner Spies and Sabine Rewald, exh. cat. (New York: Metropolitan Museum of Art, 2005), 54–55.

selected bibliography

Ades, Dawn, Krzysztof Fijalkowski, Steven Harris, Georges Sebbag, and Michael Richardson, eds. *The International Encyclopedia of Surrealism* (three vols.). London: Bloomsbury, 2019.

Ades, Dawn, and Michael Richardson, eds. *The Surrealism Reader: An Anthology of Ideas.* Chicago: University of Chicago Press, 2015.

Aragon, Louis. *Paris Peasant,* trans. Simon Watson Taylor. Cambridge, Mass.: Exact Change, 1994.

———. *Treatise on Style,* trans. Alyson Waters. Lincoln: University of Nebraska Press, 1991.

Artaud, Antonin. *Selected Writings,* ed. Susan Sontag. New York: Farrar, Straus and Giroux, 1976.

Balakian, Anna. *André Breton: Magus of Surrealism.* New York: Oxford University Press, 1971.

Bataille, Georges. *Visions of Excess: Selected Writings, 1927–1939,* ed. Allan Stoekl. Minneapolis: University of Minnesota Press, 1985.

Biro, Adam, René Passeron, et al. *Dictionnaire général du surréalisme et de ses environs.* Paris: Presses Universitaires de France, 1982.

Blachère, Jean-Claude. *Les Totems d'André Breton: Surréalisme et primitivisme littéraire.* Paris: L'Harmattan, 1996.

Breton, André. *Anthology of Black Humor,* ed. and trans. Mark Polizzotti. San Francisco: City Lights Books, 1997.

———. *Arcanum 17,* trans. Zack Rogow. Los Angeles: Sun and Moon Press, 1994.

———. *Break of Day,* trans. Mark Polizzotti and Mary Ann Caws. Lincoln: University of Nebraska Press, 1999.

———. *Communicating Vessels,* trans. Mary Ann Caws and Geoffrey T. Harris. Lincoln: University of Nebraska Press, 1990.

———. *Conversations: The Autobiography of Surrealism,* trans. Mark Polizzotti. New York: Paragon House, 1993.

———. *Free Rein,* trans. Michel Parmentier and Jacqueline d'Amboise. Lincoln: University of Nebraska Press, 1995.

———. *The Lost Steps,* trans. Mark Polizzotti. Lincoln: University of Nebraska Press, 1996.

———. *Mad Love,* trans. Mary Ann Caws. Lincoln: University of Nebraska Press, 1987.

———. *Manifestoes of Surrealism,* trans. Richard Seaver and Helen R. Lane. Ann Arbor: University of Michigan Press, 1969.

———. *Nadja,* trans. Richard Howard. New York: Grove Press, 1960.

———. *Surrealism and Painting,* trans. Simon Watson Taylor. Boston: MFA Publications, 2002.

———. *What Is Surrealism? Selected Writings,* ed. Franklin Rosemont. New York: Monad Press, 1978.

Breton, André, and Philippe Soupault. *The Magnetic Fields,* trans. Charlotte Mandell. New York: New York Review Books, 2020.

Breton, Simone. *Lettres à Denise Lévy, 1919–1929,* ed. Georgiana Colvile. Paris: Editions Joëlle Losfeld, 2005.

British Surrealism, exh. cat. London: Dulwich Picture Gallery, 2020.

Cardinal, Roger, and Robert Stuart Short. *Surrealism: Permanent Revelation.* New York: Studio Vista / Dutton, 1970.

Carrington, Leonora. *House of Fear.* New York: Dutton, 1988.

Caws, Mary Ann. *André Breton,* rev. ed. New York: Twayne, 1996.

Caws, Mary Ann, Rudolf Kuenzli, and Gwen Raaberg, eds. *Surrealism and Women.* Cambridge, Mass.: MIT Press, 1991.

Césaire, Aimé. *Return to My Native Land,* trans. John Berger and Anna Bostock. Brooklyn: Archipelago Books, 2013.

Chadwick, Whitney. *Women Artists and the Surrealist Movement.* Boston: Little, Brown / New York Graphic Society, 1985.

Chénieux-Gendron, Jacqueline, ed. *"Il y aura une fois": Une Anthologie du surréalisme.* Paris: Gallimard, 2003.

———. *Surrealism,* trans. Vivian Folkenflik. New York: Columbia University Press, 1990.

Clébert, Jean-Paul. *Dictionnaire du surréalisme.* Paris: Editions du Seuil, 1996.

D'Alessandro, Stephanie, and Matthew Gale, eds. *Surrealism Beyond Borders,* exh. cat. New York: Metropolitan Museum of Art, 2021.

Dalí, Salvador. *Le Mythe tragique de l'Angélus de Millet: Interprétation "paranoïaque-critique,"* rev. ed. Paris: Jean-Jacques Pauvert, 1978.

Dempsey, Amy. *Surrealism.* London: Thames and Hudson, 2019.

Durozoi, Gérard. *History of the Surrealist Movement,* trans. Alison Anderson. Chicago: University of Chicago Press, 2002.

4 Dada Suicides: Selected Texts of Arthur Cravan, Jacques Rigaut, Julien Torma, and Jacques Vaché. London: Atlas Press, 1995.

Gale, Matthew. *Dada and Surrealism.* London: Phaidon, 1997.

Gauthier, Xavière. *Surréalisme et sexualité.* Paris: Gallimard, 1971.

Gershman, Herbert S. *The Surrealist Revolution in France.* Ann Arbor: University of Michigan Press, 1969.

Hopkins, David. *Dada and Surrealism: A Very Short Introduction.* Oxford: Oxford University Press, 2004.

———, ed. *A Companion to Dada and Surrealism.* New York: John Wiley and Sons, 2016.

Jean, Marcel, ed. *The Autobiography of Surrealism.* New York: Viking Press, 1980.

Lautréamont [Isidore Ducasse]. *Maldoror and the Complete Works,* trans. Alexis Lykiard. Cambridge, Mass.: Exact Change, 1994.

Lewis, Helena. *The Politics of Surrealism.* New York: Paragon House, 1988.

Lippard, Lucy R., ed. *Surrealists on Art.* Englewood Cliffs, N.J.: Prentice-Hall, 1970.

Mahon, Alyce. *Surrealism and the Politics of Eros, 1938–1968.* London: Thames and Hudson, 2005.

Mundy, Jennifer, ed. *Surrealism: Desire Unbound,* exh cat. Princeton: Princeton University Press, 2001.

Nadeau, Maurice. *The History of Surrealism,* trans. Richard Howard. New York: Macmillan, 1965.

Ottinger, Didier, ed. *Dictionnaire de l'objet surréaliste.* Paris: Gallimard, 2013.

Pierre, José, ed. *Investigating Sex: Surrealist Discussions, 1928–1932,* trans. Malcolm Imrie. New York: Verso, 1992.

Polizzotti, Mark. *Revolution of the Mind: The Life of André Breton,* rev. ed. Boston: Black Widow Press, 2008.

———, ed. *André Breton: Selections.* Berkeley: University of California Press, 2003.

La Révolution surréaliste. Facsimile edition. Paris: Jean-Michel Place, 1975.

Richardson, Michael, and Krzysztof Fijalkowski, eds. *Surrealism Against the Current: Tracts and Declarations.* London: Pluto Press, 2001.

Rimbaud, Arthur. *The Drunken Boat: Selected Writings,* ed. and trans. Mark Polizzotti. New York: New York Review Books, 2022.

Rosemont, Penelope. *Surrealism: Inside the Magnetic Fields.* San Francisco: City Lights Books, 2019.

———, ed. *Surrealist Women: An International Anthology.* Austin: University of Texas Press, 1998.

Rubin, William S. *Dada, Surrealism, and Their Heritage,* exh. cat. New York: Museum of Modern Art, 1968.

Sawin, Martica. *Surrealism in Exile and the Beginning of the New York School.* Cambridge, Mass.: MIT Press, 1995.

Sebbag, Georges. *Le Surréalisme.* Paris: Editions Nathan, 1994.

Spector, Jack J. *Surrealist Art and Writing, 1919–1939: The Gold of Time.* Cambridge: Cambridge University Press, 1997.

Le Surréalisme au service de la Révolution. Facsimile edition. Paris: Jean-Michel Place, 1976.

Susik, Abigail. *Surrealist Sabotage and the War on Work.* Manchester: Manchester University Press, 2021.

Tashjian, Dickran. *A Boatload of Madmen: Surrealism and the American Avant-Garde, 1920–1950.* New York: Thames and Hudson, 1995.

Vaché, Jacques, *Lettres de guerre, 1914–1918,* ed. Patrice Allain and Thomas Guillemin. Paris: Gallimard, 2018.

Waldberg, Patrick. *Surrealism.* London: Thames and Hudson, 1997.

acknowledgments

Thirty years have passed since I wrote *Revolution of the Mind: The Life of André Breton*, its publication coinciding with the centennial of Breton's birth. Since then, I've explored a variety of topics, but Surrealism, whether directly or peripherally, has never been out of my field of vision. For *Why Surrealism Matters*, which is being published on the movement's official centennial, I have both revisited old sources and consulted many new ones. To my surprise and delight, I've discovered just how much I still had to learn about this endlessly rich and provocative movement: in its byways and crossroads, its roots and rhizomes, Surrealism remains virtually inexhaustible.

Seemingly inexhaustible, too, is the list of individuals whose wisdom and guidance have helped shaped my thinking about Surrealism over the years, many of whom I was able to thank in the acknowledgments to *Revolution of the Mind*. I'd particularly like to pay tribute to those who gave of their time and knowledge when I was researching the biography, and whose comments to me are reflected in *Why Surrealism Matters*: Leonora Carrington, Claude Courtot, Monique Fong, Mary Jayne Gold, Claude Lévi-Strauss, Edouard Roditi, and Jean Schuster.

For the present reevaluation, I owe a special debt of gratitude to the following individuals for commissioning essays, inviting me to give lectures, sharing their insights, and giving me opportunities to sharpen my thinking about this admittedly amorphous subject: Mary Ann Caws, Jacqueline Chénieux-Gendron, Stephanie D'Alessandro, Ben Downing, Marilyn Kallet, Herbert Leibowitz, Anne-Marie Levine, Chris Lyon, Samuel Reilly, Zack Rogow, Rainer Schulte, Leon Wieseltier, Trevor Winkfield, and Bill Zavatsky.

At Yale University Press, I'm grateful to John Donatich for believing in this project; to Patricia Fidler, for encouraging it; to my editor, Katherine Boller, for developing it; to Alison Hagge, for overseeing it; to David Luljak, for indexing it; to Kati Woock, for proofreading it; to Chris Crochetière, for typesetting it; to Sonia Shannon, for designing its jacket; to Sarah Henry, for producing it; and to my copy editor and longtime partner in crime, Dan Heaton, for improving it.

My deep love and thanks to Jacky Colliss Harvey, Deborah Karl, and the late Christopher Sawyer-Lauçanno for reading multiple variants of the manuscript, providing endless amounts of commentary and support, and keeping me on the right path. I owe you.

Finally, in memory of my mother, Grace Polizzotti, and of my father, Mario Polizzotti, who was lost to Covid-19 while this book was being written.

index

Mark Polizzotti's previous books include *Revolution of the Mind: The Life of André Breton*, *Bob Dylan: Highway 61 Revisited*, *Sympathy for the Traitor: A Translation Manifesto*, and *Jump Cuts: Essays on Surrealism, Film, Music, Culture, and Other Utopian Topics*. The translator of more than sixty books from the French, he directs the publications program at the Metropolitan Museum of Art.

Featuring intriguing pairings of authors and subjects, each volume in the **Why X Matters** series presents a concise argument for the continuing relevance of an important idea.

Also in the series:

Why Acting Matters	David Thomson
Why Architecture Matters	Paul Goldberger
Why Arendt Matters	Elisabeth Young-Bruehl
Why Argument Matters	Lee Siegel
Why Baseball Matters	Susan Jacoby
Why the Constitution Matters	Mark Tushnet
Why Dance Matters	Mindy Aloff
Why the Dreyfus Affair Matters	Louis Begley
Why Food Matters	Paul Freedman
Why the Museum Matters	Daniel H. Weiss
Why the New Deal Matters	Eric Rauchway
Why Niebuhr Matters	Charles Lemert
Why Poetry Matters	Jay Parini
Why Preservation Matters	Max Page
Why the Romantics Matter	Peter Gay
Why Sound Matters	Damon Krukowski
Why Translation Matters	Edith Grossman
Why Trilling Matters	Adam Kirsch
Why Writing Matters	Nicholas Delbanco